Your Total Communication Image

Your Total Communication Image

Janet Signe Olson, Ph.D.

SkillPath Publications

Mission, KS

Project Editor: Kelly Scanlon

Editor: Jane Doyle Guthrie

Page Layout: Premila Malik Borchardt and Rod Hankins

Cover Design: Rod Hankins

Library of Congress Catalog Card Number: 96-71252

ISBN: 1-57294-075-1

10   9   8   7   6   5   4   3   2   99   00   01

Printed in the United States of America

For

Robert Thurmond Carl Olson,

who taught me how to talk

and

Carl Gustav Sigurd Hammerstrom,

who taught me how to listen

Contents

Introduction

This book is intended to heighten your awareness of four communication components: PowerVoice, PowerSpeech, PowerLanguage, and PowerTalk. No matter what you may think of your communication skills right now in any of these areas, you have the ability to modify, improve, or change them. You will need the desire and determination to work toward a better communication image, and that image will help you to have a powerful impact in whatever you do.

Make this new communication image an ongoing process that you will continue to work on for many years to come. By focusing on each of the four components of your total communication image, you will develop the following specific skills:

- Your voice will be fuller and better-sounding.

- Your speech will be clearer and easier to understand.

- You will improve your ability to express your thoughts.

- You will improve your ability to present yourself and interact with others.

The purpose of *Your Total Communication Image* is to inform you of basic communication principles and to provide you with strategies for general self-improvement. If you are concerned about your voice and speech, or feel physical discomfort during any of the exercises in this book, consult your physician. He or she can determine whether you have a medical problem or whether you need to be referred to a speech-language pathologist or another specialist.

Your Total Communication Image: An Overview

Have you ever watched someone walk into a room who was good looking, well dressed, and seemed to exude self-confidence? You may have envied that person a little or thought that this was someone you'd like to get to know. As you watched, you may have formed certain impressions or opinions based on the person's physical appearance or demeanor.

When you finally heard the person speak, did your first impression change? Was the voice so shrill it felt like a nail going through your head? Perhaps the person sounded childish and insecure, or used incorrect grammar. Maybe the voice sounded okay, but you had a difficult time understanding what was said because it either sounded garbled or did not make much sense.

Does a person's communication make a difference in how you perceive him or her? If it does, you're not alone. Many of us frequently make judgments about others based not only on how they *look* but also on how they *sound*.

You may recall another instance when you were attracted to or impressed with someone who spoke well. The sound of the person's voice may have been compelling, or you wanted to know more because he or she sounded intelligent and interesting. Some people have the charisma to influence others just by using effective communication skills. The positive *communication image* that an effective communicator projects is one of the invaluable tools that you can use to get ahead and achieve your goals.

Take a few moments now and complete the Communication Image Checklist on the next page.

Communication Image Checklist

Check "Yes" or "No" for each statement below.

Yes   No

☐   ☐   1.   I avoid speaking in front of groups of people because I get nervous.

☐   ☐   2.   I form opinions of other peoples' ability levels based on their vocabulary skills.

☐   ☐   3.   Shrill voices annoy me because they are unpleasant.

☐   ☐   4.   I judge someone as less intelligent if they mispronounce words.

☐   ☐   5.   I respect a firm, commanding voice.

☐   ☐   6.   People who talk too loud are pushy.

☐   ☐   7.   People who interrupt others are rude.

☐   ☐   8.   Whenever someone mumbles, I stop listening.

☐   ☐   9.   Bad grammar is like bad manners.

☐   ☐   10. I'm attracted to people who sound confident and self-assured.

If you checked any "Yes" responses, you're probably already aware that your communication style says a great deal about you to other people. You also form opinions and make assumptions about others based on the way they communicate to you.

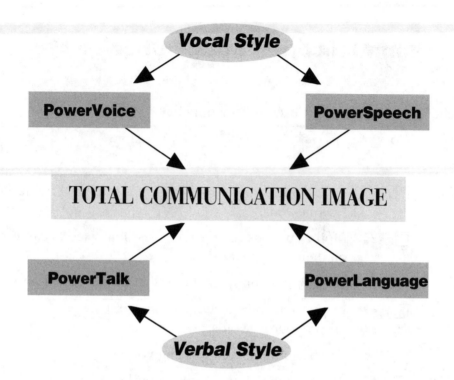

What Is Your Total Communication Image?

Your Total Communication Image includes four basic components in communication: PowerVoice, PowerSpeech, PowerLanguage, and PowerTalk. How well you use the skills in each of these areas contributes to your overall communication image. The four skill areas are divided between two basic communication styles: your *vocal* style and your *verbal* style.

Vocal Style

Your vocal style concerns how you *sound* when you speak. It is made up of two parts:

PowerVoice: How vocal quality is produced through use of proper pitch, resonance, volume, rate, and inflection. Vocal quality gives communication its emotion and personality.

PowerSpeech: How individual sounds are articulated and how these sounds are combined to make up words. The pronunciation of words is what gives communication its clarity and intelligibility.

Verbal Style

Your verbal style refers to the *message* you convey when you speak by using language and interacting with others. It is also made up of two parts:

PowerLanguage: How vocabulary, grammar, and nonverbal communication combine to communicate the actual meaning or content of the message. These aspects of language can be used to get specific, positive results.

PowerTalk: How presentation skills and interpersonal skills impact communication. It's important to consider that *how* you communicate is just as important as *what* you communicate.

Why Is Your Total Communication Image Important?

Think about the people you interact with on a regular basis. What assumptions do you make about them—family, friends, co-workers, acquaintances, and so forth—based purely on how they *sound?* Do certain individuals inspire or attract you? Or are you annoyed by the way they communicate? You might not be able to put your finger on exactly why you like or dislike someone's communication, but you may still make overall assumptions or develop an overall impression.

Your ability to communicate affects almost everything you do. Every time you speak, you are letting people know something about yourself. The way that you communicate is part of your individual personality and identity. Although you probably pay attention to the way you dress, style your hair, or decorate your home because you know that these things reveal your personal tastes, you may not be as aware that the way you communicate can also reveal just as much about you and sometimes even more.

Strong communication skills have become a very necessary part of most occupations today. Employers often rank communication skills as one of the first factors they consider when hiring new employees, and many have made considerable training investments to develop employees' proficiency in speaking and communicating. Improved communication helps you relate well to others and accomplish what you want.

The opinion you form about how a person sounds is based on that person's total communication image. Those impressions you form about others can be either positive or negative. The chart on the following page shows a sampling of some impressions that can be associated with communication skills.

Positive Impressions	Negative Impressions
authoritative	insecure
mature	childish
knowledgeable	uneducated
intelligent	unintelligent
credible	undependable
inspiring	annoying
assertive	aggressive
supportive	complaining
secure	afraid
sophisticated	dull

You can probably think of several additional descriptors yourself.

Remember: You often make judgments about others based on their ability to communicate. They also make judgments about you based on your communication skills.

Merits of Your Total Communication Image

Developing a total communication image provides you with positive results and a definite return on your investment in the effort that good communication requires. Consider the merits of effective communication:

Motivation. Effective communication allows you to gain your listeners' attention and maintain their interest. Your listeners will be motivated to hear what you have to say and will be influenced by your ability to positively meet communication challenges.

Efficiency. Increasing the accuracy and clarity of what you have to say eliminates confusion and helps to avoid mistakes. By making your communication easy for your listener to understand, you will save time, money, and effort because things will be done correctly the first time.

Relationships. You can improve your relationships at home and on the job when you communicate your thoughts and feelings more effectively. Improved communication can also help to avoid misunderstandings or resolve any conflicts that may arise.

Impact. Effective communication enables you to have a positive impact on others. This positive impact in turn adds to your credibility and professional image.

Teamwork. You can build mutual trust and respect with others by using effective communication as the path for working together. This creates an atmosphere where ideas can be shared.

Success. High-quality communication enables you to make a positive impression and gain support for what you want to accomplish. You will be able to enlist the resources you need because you will sound like you can accomplish what you want.

Assessing Your Total Communication Image

To begin to explore your total communication image, take a baseline measurement of yourself using the Communication Image Assessment on the next page.

Communication Image Assessment

Circle the number that best describes your response to each sentence (1=never, 2=rarely, 3=sometimes, 4=usually, 5=always).

1. My voice is appropriate for me.

    1   2   3   4   5

2. My voice commands respect from others.

    1   2   3   4   5

3. My voice is melodic and pleasant-sounding.

    1   2   3   4   5

4. I use appropriate volume when I speak.

    1   2   3   4   5

5. I speak at an even rate that is not too fast to understand.

    1   2   3   4   5

6. I am easily understood when I speak.

    1   2   3   4   5

7. I correctly pronounce words.

    1   2   3   4   5

8. My speech is free of articulation errors.

    1   2   3   4   5

9. My accent or regional dialect is easily understood.

    1   2   3   4   5

10. I do not slur sounds or drop endings from words.

    1   2   3   4   5

11. People understand me without my needing to reword what I say.

    1   2   3   4   5

12. My choice of words is always accurate and concise.

    1   2   3   4   5

13. I have a large vocabulary and use it when I speak.

    1   2   3   4   5

14. I use correct grammar when I speak.

    1   2   3   4   5

15. I avoid offending or insulting others when I speak.

    1   2   3   4   5

16. I am a good listener.

    1   2   3   4   5

17. I am confident making speeches and presentations.

    1   2   3   4   5

18. Other people pay attention to what I say.

    1   2   3   4   5

19. I am confident about my conversational skills.

    1   2   3   4   5

20. I contribute to another person's topic of conversation.

    1   2   3   4   5

Your Total Score: _____

80 to 100	Excellent	Work to maintain your communication skills.
60 to 79	Good	Polish and refine your communication skills.
40 to 59	Fair	Add to your communication skills by using the suggestions in this book.
0 to 39	Need to Improve	Work to develop your communication skills by following the suggestions in this book.

As you work through this book, you can come back to this assessment periodically to determine how you have changed and improved.

Fundamentals of Your Total Communication Image

Success is always grounded in a good beginning. Starting with the right essentials will allow you to build your communication image on a solid foundation that provides both the necessary prerequisites and the critical skills for continued success and growth. The PowerTips in this chapter will set you on the right course of action and give you skills and practices that you can use in your everyday life. Learning these elements well from the start will give you a base on which to build and learn.

PowerPlan

To build a base for the fundamentals of communication, you need to:

1. *Get ready for change.*

2. *Learn relaxation techniques.*

3. *Use correct posture.*

4. *Learn proper breathing techniques.*

5. *Practice good vocal hygiene.*

PowerTip #1: Get Ready for Change

The way you communicate is a very personal part of you. When you change your communication style, you are changing a part of yourself, and that can be uncomfortable at first. When you were a child, you learned speech and vocal patterns that you in turn used to communicate with others. These learned patterns were reinforced and, over time, became second nature to you. Before you can change how you communicate, first take a look at why you use the patterns that you do now. There are factors that influence what you do and why you continue to use certain patterns over and over.

Factors That Influence Communication

The social pressures and stereotypes that exist in your life may contribute to your communication patterns—and you may not even realize it is happening. Do you feel there are certain things you must do to maintain a certain role? For example, do you think you should sound like a quiet, feminine woman who is submissive to her husband, family, and boss? Or perhaps that you should sound like a strong, masculine male who is ready for any fight that may come along? If the answer is "yes," you may be responding to old stereotypes of what society once expected of males and females and how they sounded or communicated to those around them. Sometimes you may speak in a way you think you should in order to fit into the society around you.

Flawed communication habits also may result from not knowing what to do. Lack of information can cause you to use improper techniques in speaking or prevent you from changing bad practices, simply because you don't know how to change or improve them. Once you know what to do, you can build up those skills that aren't working well for you. The discussions that follow will show you how.

Habits are actions that feel natural, even though they might not present the best way of doing something. You may find it difficult to change at first because new ways of doing things often seem unnatural or awkward until they become new habits. The new pattern then becomes something you can do without thinking about it.

Your environment also influences how you communicate. If your usual home or work surroundings are noisy, you must compete to be heard, and this may affect how you communicate. Certain physical conditions such as dryness of the air in the room or exposure to chemical elements also have an impact on how you sound, and in turn on how you communicate.

Preparing for Change

In preparing for change, you may have to make some decisions. Change will require that you learn some new information and then apply that knowledge in ways you may not be doing now. Ask yourself the following questions to determine how motivated you are to make changes:

Should you change?

- Is there something about your communication that's not working for you?

- Will changing your communication image help you in some way?

- Is now the right time to be considering a change?

Do you want to change?

- Is the decision to change one that you made for yourself?

- Is something in your life standing in your way?

- Are you committed to working for this change?

How do you want to change?

- Do you want to change your entire communication image?

- Do you want to modify or improve a part of your communication image?

- Do you want to unlearn or eliminate old practices and habits?

If you answered "yes" to any of these questions, you're ready for change. This process can be fun and exciting, and may lead you to new possibilities and ways of communicating. Once you have decided to change something about yourself, you need an overall plan of action. This will allow you to adjust to the changes that occur so that they become a natural part of you.

The Three Ps of Change

When you change your Total Communication Image, you need to keep in mind that it involves three elements: practice, patience, and persistence.

Practice

- **Set a schedule and follow it as closely as you can.** Aim for practicing fifteen to twenty minutes every day, or scatter five-minute practice sessions throughout the day.

- **Work on one objective at a time so that your efforts are concentrated.** You will avoid becoming confused, and you will learn each concept thoroughly.

- **Work alone in a quiet spot.** This way you can think about what you are doing and try new techniques without feeling uncomfortable or conspicuous.

Patience

- **Work slowly and proceed at your own rate.** You are doing this work to benefit yourself, not to please someone else. Take as much time as you need for each skill.

- **Be open to feeling self-conscious at first.** You may sound different, and with that you may feel awkward. Practice will make you comfortable with your new communication image.

- **Give yourself time to accept small, gradual changes instead of expecting an instantaneous dramatic change.** By learning in small steps, you will integrate these changes more easily than if you try to sound completely different all at once.

Persistence

- **Be consistent in how and when you practice.** By setting up a schedule and following it, you will train yourself to practice and use the new skills in a standardized manner.

- **Use a visual or tactile reminder to help you continue your practice.** Wear a ring or small bandage, for example. and touch it during the day to help you remember to use these new communication skills.

- **Build usage with other people slowly.** First try your new skills with a partner or supporter who knows what you're trying to do; then expand the circle to include family, friends, co-workers, and others.

PowerTip #2: Learn Relaxation Techniques

You can do everything better when you're relaxed. Tension can collect in different parts of your body and affect how you sound. Tension creates strain on your muscles, particularly the small ones associated with vocal and speech production, and it can affect your breathing, making your voice sound harsh and choppy.

Learn to relax and get rid of the tension that may be affecting how you sound. Releasing this tension will give your voice a rich, full sound instead of one that is strained or limited in some way. Try these relaxation exercises:

- **Yawn and sigh.** Inhale and take a deep breath. Open your mouth wide and give a big yawn. Sigh softly until all the air is gone from your lungs. Repeat several times.

- **Do head rolls.** Drop your head forward and let your chin rest on your chest. Gently roll your head around in a complete circle starting to the left. Then roll in a complete circle in the opposite direction. Finally, raise your head and look straight ahead. Lower your left ear toward your left shoulder, raise your head to the starting position, and repeat by lowering your right ear toward your right shoulder.

- **Perform shoulder rolls.** Roll your shoulders in a circle starting toward the front and moving to the back; then reverse the direction. Next, raise your shoulders up toward your ears as high as you can go. Lower and repeat several times.

- **Do face scrunches.** Scrunch your face together in a pucker as hard as you can. Next, open your eyes and mouth as wide as they will go. Finally, relax your entire face. Feel the tension leave your eyes, lips, nose, cheeks, and jaw.

- **Stretch your body.** Stretch your entire body using yoga stretches or by doing simple stretching exercises for your arms, legs, and back.

- **Listen to sounds around you.** Sit quietly, close your eyes, and listen to soothing music or just the noises around you. Concentrate on the sounds that you hear.

- **Watch yourself.** Watch yourself in a mirror. Look for facial tensions and mannerisms that may keep you from relaxing fully.

- **Get plenty of exercise.** Walk or do some low-impact aerobic activity that releases tension and encourages good breathing habits.

- **Retreat from stress.** Give yourself some down time and retreat from the world for a few minutes. Put your thumbs in your ears to block out noise and place your fingers over your eyes to block out light. Take deep breaths and visualize a favorite scene.

- **Eat a balanced diet.** Avoid excess sugar and caffeine, both of which can tend to make you feel irritable and jumpy.

PowerTip #3: Use Correct Posture

Correct posture provides the physical support that gives your voice and speech their strength and fullness. Without good support, you cannot sustain even the best techniques. Good posture literally supports the vocal mechanism and allows it to function properly. Good posture also allows your body to oxygenate itself and your organs to do what they are supposed to.

Your carriage provides a visual impact to your Total Communication Image. Slumped posture conveys a passive or sloppy appearance that may color how others perceive you when you speak. By standing erect, you can portray the self-confidence necessary to project a positive communication image. Don't let poor posture belie your words and cloud what good habits you already have.

Make it a habit to practice correct posture whether you're sitting, standing, or walking. Using good posture will provide the physical support you need and also help to reduce the fatigue that can result from tension created by improper body positions.

General Suggestions for Posture

No matter what you're doing, particularly avoid slouching—it affects the back of your neck, your throat, and your breathing mechanism.

Remember to practice these important elements of good posture:

- Head up
- Chin out
- Neck straight
- Shoulders back
- Back straight
- Stomach in

If you use the telephone for a prolonged time, don't cradle the phone between your chin and shoulder. This positioning can cause tension and cramping in your neck and throat. Instead, hold the telephone with your hand or use a headset or speaker phone so your neck and head can assume a more natural position.

Practice walking with good posture while pushing a shopping cart. The cart will help you balance yourself as you walk. Practice with your back straight and your stride smooth and even.

When You Are Sitting

When you are sitting, use the *double bend* position. You will appear balanced, and your body will be supported properly. This position also helps you to look slimmer! Here's how:

- Sit fully on the chair, bending at your hips.
- Bend your knees so that your feet rest flat on the floor.
- Don't cross your legs—it interferes with circulation and balance.
- Place your hands on your thighs to keep your shoulders back, or put your hands on the arms of the chair.

When You Are Standing

Keep your weight on both feet. This will distribute your weight evenly and avoid putting too much stress on one hip and leg. It will also help to protect your back from strain and pulling to one side.

Keep your body aligned as though there is a string going up through the center of your torso to the top of your head. This will make you look symmetrical and balanced.

Use a *parade rest* position to stand: clasp your hands behind your back and stand with your weight on both feet. This posture works well if you have a habit of putting your hands in your pockets or slouching to one side. It also keeps your shoulders back.

PowerTip #4: Learn Proper Breathing Techniques

Because you breathe automatically, you may not have given how you do it much thought. However, breathing properly for your voice and speech is a conscious process. Proper breathing supports the vocal mechanism and allows you to project your voice in a clear, strong manner. Shallow breathing does not support the voice, and when done for an extended period of time, can actually cause fatigue (it makes your body tense up). Learning abdominal breathing will give you endurance and give your voice more power. It will also help to keep you calm and to project a more confident communication image. Here is what proper breathing does for you:

- It allows you to use proper voice and speech production. Before you speak, you inhale, and then you talk on the air expelled.

- It helps you to relax so that you can project the calm impression that you are in control.

- It keeps your voice vibrant and guards against fading out at the end of a sentence.

- It reduces tension and fatigue by keeping your body supplied with enough oxygen.

Learn Correct Breathing Patterns

Try the following exercises in order to enhance your breathing patterns. The more you practice these each day, the more automatic good breathing habits will become. And the better your breathing habits, the more your communication image will improve.

- **Learn abdominal breathing.** Sit in a chair or lie down and put one hand on your chest and the other on your abdomen. Breath in through your nose and completely fill your lungs. The hand on your chest should stay still while the one on your abdomen should rise up as the latter expands. Blow out the air through your mouth, and let the hand on your abdomen come back down as your abdominal muscles contract. Repeat several breathing cycles this way.

- **Breathe in slow cycles.** Take a deep breath through your nose for a count of four. Hold the breath for a count of two, then slowly blow the air out of your mouth for a count of four. Repeat this cycle three times.

- **Build stamina.** Take a deep breath and count out loud for as long as you can on that one breath. Each time you try this exercise, try to count to a higher number.

PowerTip #5: Practice Good Vocal Hygiene

Practicing good vocal hygiene means taking care of your vocal mechanism and avoiding habits or substances that may cause harm to these structures. The most important task is taking care of your *vocal folds*, the two delicate membranes located in your *larynx* (or voice box) that shorten and elongate to produce different pitches. Male vocal folds are longer and thicker than the female variety, which usually makes the male voice lower in pitch.

Harmful vocal habits may cause irritation or strain on your vocal folds, resulting in temporary or even permanent damage. This damage can make your voice sound gruff or hoarse, or may cause you to lose your voice altogether. Prolonged vocal abuse can cause blisters to form on the folds, which then may callous over into harder surfaces called nodules. Changes in the surface of the vocal folds can alter the sound of your voice. By practicing good vocal hygiene, you help keep your voice in top condition.

Factors That Affect Good Vocal Hygiene

Good vocal hygiene means avoiding any practices or substances that can create problems for the vocal mechanism. Preventing vocal misuse and abuse will help your voice stay vital and strong. You should try to eliminate any abuse or at least modify what is under your control to avoid problems in the future. The better you take care of your vocal mechanism, the better your voice will sound. The following chart outlines the elements of poor vocal hygiene.

Elements of Poor Vocal Hygiene

Physical Actions	Vocal folds can be forced together harshly and can thicken if they are irritated or dried out.
Examples:	• Frequent throat clearing • Strong coughing • Heavy lifting • Mouth breathing
Suggestions:	• Instead of clearing your throat or coughing, pant like a dog and then swallow. • Avoid heavy lifting, which puts strain on the vocal folds. • Reduce nasal congestion and breathe through your nose.

Improper Vocalizing	Overusing or abusing your voice strains vocal folds and causes inflammation.
Examples:	• Yelling or loud talking • Loud whispering • Pitch that is consistently too high or too low • Sustained talking
Suggestions:	• Time your vocalizations around loud noise to minimize yelling and straining. • Use other methods to get someone's attention, such as flicking a light, in order to avoid loud speech. • Instead of a monotone, vary your pitch so that you use more of your vocal range.

Environment	Environmental conditions and exposure to substances and toxic elements can dry out and irritate the vocal folds.
Examples:	• Air pollution, pollen, and dust • Fumes and smoke • Cold air and air conditioning • Working around loud machinery and music
Suggestions:	• Avoid areas that are polluted with dust, pollen, and substances such as smoke and fumes. • Use hand signals or signs to avoid talking over loud noise. • Use a humidifier if the air in the room is too dry.

Medical Factors	Physical conditions and disorders can cause irritation. Chronic stress produces tightening of the vocal folds.
Examples:	• Allergies and sinus problems • Colds and flu • Tension, fatigue, and stress • Medications such as aspirin
Suggestions:	• Get plenty of rest to avoid fatigue and reduce tension and stress. • Exercise and practice relaxation techniques. • Use medications wisely.

Diet and Lifestyle	Various substances can dry out and irritate the vocal folds or cause excess mucous to form. Extreme temperatures in hot or cold liquids and/or cigarettes cause tension.
Examples:	• Smoking • Alcohol and caffeine • Extremes in hot or cold beverages • Dairy products and chocolate
Suggestions:	• Drink plenty of water to keep the throat lubricated and use lozenges if your throat is dry. • Monitor your diet for foods that can create excess mucous, such as cheese, milk, or chocolate. • Stop smoking or at least try to cut down. Also limit your exposure to secondhand smoke because this too can dry out your throat and vocal folds.

Power Exercise

The first step in improving your Total Communication Image is to develop good listening skills. The following PowerExercises will help you start building these skills so that you can use them throughout all the exercises in this book. Train yourself to listen, so that you will be able to apply what you learn about improving the way you speak.

1. Make your own communication tape.

Make a tape recording of yourself while doing something routine such as talking to a friend on the phone or having a conversation during dinner. Listen to this tape to get an idea of how you *really* sound in casual conversation. (You also will refer to this recording as you complete exercises in the other chapters of this book.) Use a tape recorder that runs on household AC power if possible because varying battery power may distort the recording of voice qualities such as pitch, rate, and inflection.

2. Learn to listen to yourself.

Listen to yourself and pay attention to how you sound at different times of the day, in different situations, and while talking to different people. Identify what you like and don't like about your communication patterns. Try the following techniques to get a fairly accurate idea of how you sound without using a tape recorder. These methods help to bounce your voice back to you so that you can hear how you sound to others.

- Read aloud holding an open book close to your face. Talk into the fold of the book.

- Stand in the corner of a room and talk into the corner. If the walls are ceramic tile, that's even better, because your voice will be reflected rather than absorbed.

- Put your thumbs underneath your chin and cup your fingers behind your ears. Pull your ears forward and talk.

3. Find role models.

Listen to other people and identify what you like about their communication style. You may find a role model in a friend, family member, co-worker, or perhaps a professional television or radio speaker. Pick someone whose communication you admire and identify elements of his or her style that you may want to try for yourself.

4. Keep a communication log.

A log will allow you to keep a diary of your activities for improvement and a record of your progress. You may want to record your activities with the Communication Log provided on the next page. Just like the tape, you can use this format as you work through other exercises in this book. Doing so will let you see what you've already done, where you are now, and where you need to go.

Communication Log

Date	Activity	Observations and Notes

3

PowerVoice: Improving Your Vocal Quality

Your voice forms an essential part of your Total Communication Image. It reveals so much about you to others because it reflects your emotional state and physical condition. Even your personality comes through your vocal quality.

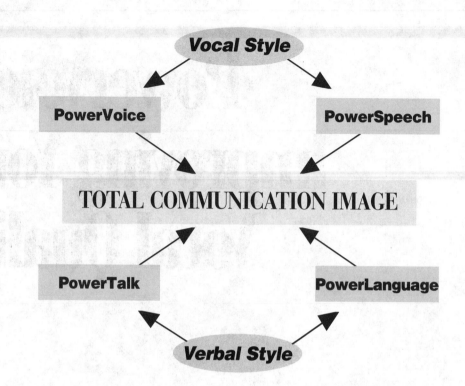

A voice that embodies good vocal qualities will motivate people to listen. Conversely, a voice that contains negative qualities will interfere with communication because it may sound irritating or lifeless. Improving your voice can be as simple as learning a few techniques that will improve your vocal production.

PowerPlan

To improve your vocal quality, be sure to use correct:

1. **Pitch.**

2. **Resonance.**

3. **Volume.**

4. **Rate.**

5. **Inflection and stress.**

PowerTip #1: Pitch

Pitch refers to how high or low your voice sounds and is determined by how fast or slowly your vocal folds vibrate. The more tension you put on your vocal folds, the faster they vibrate and the higher the pitch becomes. This explains why your pitch tends to rise whenever you get excited. When you're relaxed, your pitch will become somewhat lower due to less tension on the vocal folds and throat muscles.

The length, thickness, and density of your vocal folds also affect your pitch. Men generally have lower voices, vibrating anywhere from 60 to 260 cycles per second, while women usually have higher-pitched voices, ranging from about 100 to 525 cycles per second. The pitch of your voice is determined primarily by the physical size and condition of your vocal folds, but there are also some other important issues to note concerning your pitch.

Stereotypes or prejudices often exist regarding pitch, and these tend to influence how other people perceive you. For example, if you consistently speak in a pitch that seems too high for you, others could perceive you as immature or unsure of yourself. A high pitch may conjure up an image of a "helpless little girl" who needs someone to take care of her. On the other hand, a pitch that's too low can make you come across as dull or lacking in energy (though sometimes people use a lower pitch thinking it creates an image of authority). In either case, a pitch that's too high or too low can sound annoying. Continually using an improper pitch also can cause stress on the vocal folds, which may lead to physical problems such as nodules or vocal strain.

How Your Pitch Differs

Habitual pitch is the pitch you use most frequently when you speak. Though your habitual pitch may feel completely natural because it's how you normally sound, it may not be the best one for you. You may be unknowingly using a pitch level that's either too high or too low. Alternatively, perhaps you're purposely using an improper pitch level to project an image of how you think you should sound. Either way, using an incorrect pitch level is neither healthy for your voice nor will it help you develop your best vocal image.

Optimum pitch level is the level that's best for you. It's determined by your own physical structures and the ease with which you can produce the sound. Using your optimum pitch level will enable you to use your voice to its fullest capability without contributing to vocal fatigue. At first you may feel awkward with this optimum pitch level if it's not the one you routinely use.

Pitch range refers to the variety of pitches that you use. Normal speech requires that you vary your pitch range whenever you speak. That is, just as you would not sing a one-note song, you should not speak exclusively at one pitch. Doing so would make you sound monotonous and would quickly put others to sleep. Instead, you should employ a range of pitches when you speak in order to add interest to your voice. You tend to raise your pitch when you ask a question or emphasize a word, and you tend to lower it at the end of a statement or when you want to create a little drama. Varying pitch can add to the attractiveness of your voice and make you sound more energetic. The color and vibrancy that results from varying your pitch gives your voice its depth and personality.

Finding Your Optimum Pitch

Try the following exercise to find your optimum pitch level and pitch range. You may use a piano or pitch pipe, or simply do this "by ear."

1. With a *relaxed* voice, sing down the scale note by note to the lowest note you can comfortably reach.

2. Now sing up the scale four notes from the bottom. This is typically where your optimum pitch level should be. Sing "la" at this pitch several times and then start talking at this pitch level.

3. Concentrate on how this pitch sounds and feels to you. Remember, it may feel a little unnatural at first, particularly if you've been habitually using an incorrect pitch.

4. Practice speaking a note above and a note below this level to determine if a slightly higher or lower level sounds and feels more natural. You may have to adjust your pitch level a little to find the one that is right for you.

5. When you speak at this new pitch level, also use several notes below and above it as your pitch range. This will add color and interest to your voice.

6. Listen to the communication tape that you recorded in Chapter 2 and pay special attention to the pitch levels and ranges that you hear yourself using. Answer these questions:

- Does your pitch sound too high or too low?

- Do you sound like someone who is self-confident?

- Do you think that your pitch level is appropriate for you?

- Do you vary your pitch range to make it interesting?

PowerTip #2: Resonance

Resonance occurs when sound is amplified and modified to produce different tones. When you were a child, you probably experimented with blowing across the top of a soda bottle to make different-sounding tones. The variety of sounds possible depended on the size and shape of the bottle and how much you filled it with water. These sounds that you made were *resonated* by the different sizes and shapes of bottles that you used.

Vocal resonance results in much the same way, due to the cavities of your vocal tract. Your resonators are your larynx, throat cavity, sinus cavities, oral cavity, and nasal cavities. As these resonators change in size and shape, they can change the quality of the tone. When you are using good resonance, your voice should have a warm and rounded sound.

One of the most important types of resonance that affects your voice is *nasal resonance*. This occurs when air vibrates in your nasal cavities and slightly escapes through your nose. Say the consonants *m, n,* and *ng* (as in *ring*), and feel the mild buzzing sensation in the bridge of your nose. These consonants are resonated in the nasal area. Two basic problems can occur with nasal resonance.

Nasality results from using excessive resonance through the nose when you speak. Too much air escapes through your nose, making your voice sound whiny and tinny. In doing this, you may create the impression that you're complaining even when that's not the case. To determine whether you sound too nasal, try a little test. Hold a mirror right under your nose and read the following sentence:

Mike had many more months to go on his mortgage.

Look at the mirror—it should have two small cloudy spots. Now, wipe off the mirror and hold it under your nose again as you read this sentence:

We walked to the store to get a loaf of bread.

Look at the mirror again. If you see any cloudiness, you could be letting air escape from your nose when it should not—meaning you sound too nasal. Using your mirror, read both sentences several times each. Try to feel and see the difference between the degrees of nasality that you use.

Denasality is caused by insufficient nasal resonance, so that little or no air escapes through the nose when you speak. You usually sound denasal when you have a cold because the nasal and sinus cavities are affected. If your nasal passages are clogged, air does not resonate properly. Your voice may sound dull and flat because it lacks resonance to give it warmth and fullness. To determine whether you are too denasal, try this test. Hold the index finger of your left hand along the side of your nose and the index finger of your right hand against your throat. Now read these words:

make   meet   might   most   must

You should feel vibrations equally in both index fingers. If you do not feel any vibrations with your left finger along the side your nose, you are probably not using enough nasal resonance.

Developing Good Resonance

Using good resonance requires a balance of resonance between your mouth and nose, known as speaking in the *mask*. The mask is the triangular-shaped area formed by the bridge of your nose and the two corners of your mouth. The term comes from ancient Greece, when actors held up a mask to present different characters and projected their voices through this façade.

When you speak through your mask, you are equally resonating sounds in your mouth, nose, and oral cavities. Your voice should sound clear, not muffled or nasal.

Make a triangle by joining both index fingers and thumbs together. Place your fingers over your face, with the index fingers at the top of the bridge of your nose and your thumbs placed under your chin. Now count from one to ten and feel the vibrations in your face. If you are speaking through your mask properly, you should feel vibrations in your nose, cheekbones, and mouth. When you speak, try to center the resonance in the mask area to give your voice a well-rounded and pleasing sound.

Try the following exercises to ensure that you're using proper resonance. Pay attention to making sounds in the mask area.

Using resonance with vowels. Say these consonants with each of the vowel sounds. Feel the vibrations in your nose, cheek, and mouth areas.

Using resonance in words. Now read these words. You may want to tape yourself and listen to how you sound. Be sure to balance the vibrations between your nasal and oral cavities so that you're not too nasal or denasal.

M	N	NG
may	neigh	anger
me	knee	shingle
my	nye	trying
moat	note	following
mew	new	doing
mat	gnat	language
met	net	strength
mitt	knit	singer
mutt	nut	rung
moss	long	stronger

Using resonance in sentences. Read the following sentences and listen to how you sound. Check again to make sure that you're balancing your resonance so that you're neither too nasal nor denasal.

43

1. Mary may want to go swimming in the summer.

2. May I join you for dinner tonight?

3. We went shopping at the mall yesterday.

4. The nightclub singer sang a song last night.

5. Michael is lifting weights to make his muscles stronger.

6. What time are you going to the museum?

7. The attorney listened to the woman give her statement.

8. She never would have gone to the movies alone.

9. Susan dialed the wrong telephone number.

10. Do you know the difference between mink and fox fur?

PowerTip #3: Volume

Volume—that is, how loud your voice sounds—is controlled by the amount of force or energy applied to the production of sound coming from your vocal tract. You generally have a regulating ability to judge how loudly you are speaking. Obviously, if you don't speak loudly enough, people will tend to say "Huh?" to you a lot. They may even perceive you as having low self-esteem or being shy. If you tend to speak too loudly, others may think you're a little overbearing. Constant loud speech can be a habit, but it also can indicate a possible hearing loss. You can use the volume level of your voice to enhance your vocal image. Consider what volume can do for you:

Add variety to your speech. Listeners tire from hearing the same volume level all the time. Changing the levels slightly from time to time will help keep your voice interesting.

Create dramatic interest. Suddenly dropping your volume to a low level or even a whisper can draw in your listeners. They will have to pay closer attention in order to hear what you're saying.

Adapt your speech. You may need to adapt to different speaking environments because of the size, shape, or acoustics of a room. As your audience grows, you will need a louder volume so that everyone can hear you.

Help you to be heard. Extraneous noises such as traffic, loud music, machinery, or even other people talking will make it necessary for you to adapt your volume level to compensate for these distractions.

Projecting Your Voice

It would seem obvious, at first, that all you have to do to raise your volume level is simply talk louder. That's the simple solution, but one that could lead to problems if you do it too much. Just remember the last time you cheered for your favorite sports team and woke up with a sore throat the next morning. That type of vocal abuse can cause strain on the vocal folds and tire the muscles in the throat, causing you some discomfort. Usually just resting your voice for a day or so returns your voice to normal. However, prolonged shouting can lead to more serious, chronic conditions like vocal nodules, which may in turn require more aggressive forms of treatment.

Louder volume is better accomplished through proper projection of the voice. Projection refers to using proper breath support to produce a louder tone. When you use projection, you can raise the volume level of your voice and avoid strain to your vocal mechanism. Your voice will be heard at a greater distance without excessively straining your vocal folds. Proper projection requires three main elements:

- *Correct posture.* You must support your breathing apparatus in order for your organs to function correctly.

- *Breath control.* You need sufficient air in order to support the louder volume.

- *Abdominal control.* You need to keep the abdominal muscles tight when releasing the air so that it's forced out with more pressure.

Try the Projection Exercise on the next page as you work on improving this aspect of your voice.

Projection Exercise

Try the following to improve the projection of your voice. Remember to make your voice louder, but don't raise your pitch level.

1. Sit up straight in a chair and take a deep breath. As you exhale, say "Ah" and try these different variations of loudness. Concentrate on making only the volume levels change, not your pitch level. Remember to tighten your abdominals as you exhale.

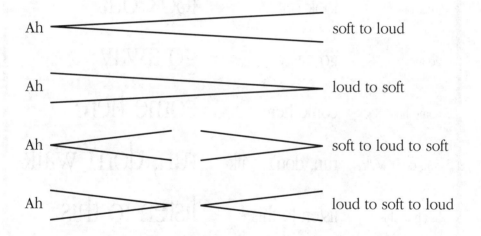

Ah   soft to loud

Ah   loud to soft

Ah   soft to loud to soft

Ah   loud to soft to loud

2. Count to the highest number you can in one breath. Use your abdominal muscles to help you control the exhalation of air in an even flow. Each time you do this exercise, try to count to a higher number.

3. Take a deep breath and part your lips slightly. Let the sound of "s" escape gently from between your teeth. See how many seconds you can make this sound before running out of air. You can try this same exercise by making the sound of "z." Try each time to make the sounds for a longer period of time.

4. Say these phrases as though you were talking from a second-story window to someone who is:

Under the window	15 feet away	30 feet away
look out	look out	look out
go away	go away	go away
come here	come here	come here
run, don't walk	run, don't walk	run, don't walk
listen to this	listen to this	listen to this
goodbye now	goodbye now	goodbye now

PowerTip #4: Rate

The rate of speech is the speed or tempo at which words are spoken in a given time frame. You usually vary your rate from time to time depending on the situation and the speaking task at hand. If you typically talk faster than people can listen, or drawl out speech at a snail's pace, you should think about modifying your rate of speech so you can be more easily understood.

It's interesting to listen to a speaker who uses slightly different speeds of speech because this technique creates variety and helps hold your attention. You don't tire as easily when you hear variety in the auditory message. If you stay within a general range when you speak, you allow others to pace themselves when they listen to you. There are some basic rates to keep in mind so that you don't speak either too quickly or too slowly for your listeners.

Rate of speech is measured in words per minute (wpm), and general conversation produces around 100 to 150 wpm. You speak more slowly if you're collecting your thoughts and faster if you're rattling off details. Newscasters speak at a faster rate of 175 wpm or higher because they have to relay quite a bit of information in a thirty-minute broadcast. Following are some speeds to keep in mind and some perceptions and considerations that occur at the opposite extremes of the speed continuum.

Rates of Speech

Slow speech (100 wpm and fewer)	Average Speech (140 wpm)	Fast speech (175 wpm and more)

◄───►

Listeners:

Can lose interest	Become fatigued
Let their minds wander	Miss details
Become bored	Become confused

Speaker appears:

Relaxed and calm	Tense or nervous
Serious	Frivolous
Tired	Energetic

Use when explaining:

Difficult information	Less important facts
Separate details	Summary information
New information	Review information

Use of Pauses

Your rate of speech is also affected by the use of pauses. The more pauses you insert in your speech, the slower your speech will be perceived. Pauses are very necessary and useful in your speech and should be used creatively to accomplish the following:

- *Give the listener time to think.* If you speak rapidly with no pauses, your listener can't absorb everything you say. Silence can be golden when you allow your listener time to think about what you are saying.

- *Show confidence and control.* Confident speakers pause during speaking. They don't rush through what they are saying in order to get finished, but rather they savor and enjoy their words.

- *Add emphasis and drama.* Effective use of pauses can create dramatic tension and motivate the listener to anticipate what you will say next. What follows after a pause is often the important part of the statement.

- *Aid comprehension of material.* Information that is detailed or difficult to understand is best presented at a slower rate. For example, when you give a phone number you should pause after the first three numbers: "My number is 555 (pause) 0000."

Phrasing

Phrasing groups words together and allows pauses to occur naturally. When you speak or read aloud, you use phrasing to join words so they don't sound isolated and choppy. Phrasing allows you to catch your breath between words and to avoid sounding like you're speaking one long, run-on sentence. When you read aloud, you usually use punctuation marks such as commas, colons, and periods to serve as guides to phrasing.

When professional readers mark a script, they will often indicate places to stop for pauses either to create an effect or simply to catch a breath. Commonly a diagonal line serves to indicate phrasing and perhaps where a slight pause should occur. An asterisk indicates that the speaker can take a breath. Try this sample reading in order to practice phrasing, pauses, and breathing patterns. After reading the passage a few times the way it's marked, try your own phrasing and pause patterns to see what works for you.

*/Speaking at a slower rate of speed/ may help you to make yourself/ more easily understood by others. */This is especially true / whenever you are speaking in a very noisy environment. */If there is much confusion/ or competing noise in the room */ other people will be able to follow what you are saying / if you do not talk too quickly. */ If your speech is too fast/ others may get confused/ or even become frustrated with what you are saying. */ Remember / keep your speed down/ if you want others to get your message/ and think that you are an accomplished speaker.

To practice rate, pauses, and phrasing, read the following passage aloud. This text, entitled "Rainbow Passage," has been used for many years by researchers to evaluate speech production. All the sounds in American English are found in this text in approximately the same proportion that you use them in everyday speech. It should take between two and two and a half minutes to read this selection.

Rainbow Passage

When the sunlight strikes raindrops in the air, they act like a prism and form a rainbow. The rainbow is a division of white light into many beautiful colors. These take the shape of a long round arch, with its path high above and its two ends apparently beyond the horizon. There is, according to legend, a boiling pot of gold at one end. People look, but no one ever finds it. When a man looks for something beyond his reach, his friends say he is looking for the pot of gold at the end of the rainbow.

Throughout the centuries, men have explained the rainbow in various ways. Some have accepted it as a miracle without physical explanation. To the Hebrews it was a token that there would be no more universal floods. The Greeks used to imagine that it was a sign from the gods to foretell war or heavy rain. The Norsemen considered the rainbow as a bridge over which the gods passed from earth to their home in the sky. Other men have tried to explain the phenomenon physically. Aristotle thought that the rainbow was caused by reflection of the sun's rays by the rain. Since then physicists have found that it is not reflection, but refraction by the raindrops, which causes the rainbow. Many complicated ideas about the rainbow have been formed. The difference in the rainbow depends considerably upon the size of the water drops, and the width of the colored band increases as the size of the drops increases. The actual primary rainbow observed is said to be the effect of superposition of a number of bows. If the red of the second bow falls upon the green of the first, the result is to give a bow with an abnormally wide yellow band, since red and green light when mixed form yellow. This is a very common type of bow, one showing mainly red and yellow, with little or no green or blue.

Source: Grant Fairbanks, Voice and Articulation Drillbook (New York: Harper & Brothers), 1940.

PowerTip #5: Stress and Intonation

Have you ever seen a science fiction movie about how robots will take over the world? Their voices give you an idea of how you would sound if you talked without using stress and intonation. Monotone, flat voices create a lifeless impression devoid of emotion and personality. Speech without stress and intonation is not interesting, and it quickly bores your listeners. Both of these vocal qualities add color and lilt to your speech and give your voice its unique personality. Your manner of using stress and intonation can be your own trademark because you can communicate in a personal, yet dramatic way. You can project an image of energy that makes what you say easier to understand.

Stress is the change in loudness that occurs by accenting part of a word or an entire word in a sentence. It helps you communicate effectively by offering a means by which you can specify, clarify, and reinforce what you want to say. If you said, "He *wanted* to leave tomorrow," you would be communicating a different meaning than, "He wanted to leave *tomorrow*." You convey ideas more specifically when you use stress (emphasis) because it focuses your listener's attention on the important part of your message. Try the Stress Exercise on the next page to give yourself a clear idea of how to implement this strategy.

Stress Exercise

Practice these exercises using different stress levels. Read each exercise aloud and say the letter or words that are in bold louder than the rest of the exercise. You should be able to hear differences in what you are saying.

Stressing sounds. Each sequence of letters should be read differently according to the letters that are stressed. This exercise will get you started using different stress patterns.

a-b   a-**b**

a-b-c   a-**b**-c   a-b-**c**

a-b-c-d   a-**b**-c-d   a-b-**c**-d   a-b-c-**d**

a-b-c-d-e   a-**b**-c-d-e   a-b-**c**-d-e   a-b-c-**d**-e   a-b-c-d-**e**

a-b   **c**-d   **e**-f   **g**-h-   **i**-j   **k**-l

a-b-c   **d**-e-f   **g**-h-i   **j**-k-l

a-b-c-d   **e**-f-g-h   **i**-j-k-l

a-b-c-**d**-e-f   **g**-h-i-**j**-k-l

Stressing words. You can change the meaning of a word by simply stressing different syllables. Read each pair of words and hear the difference between using the word as a noun or as a verb.

Noun	Verb
content	con**tent**
contest	con**test**
envelope	en**vel**ope
insult	in**sult**
object	ob**ject**
permit	per**mit**
record	re**cord**
research	re**search**
survey	sur**vey**
suspect	sus**pect**

Stressing within sentences. Change the overall meanings of these sentences by varying the stress on individual words. Each time you read the sentence, emphasize a different word to convey a different meaning. For example, "I am not going today" can be read as these different variations:

I am not going today.

I **am** not going today.

I am **not** going today.

I am not **going** today.

I am not going **today**.

Now try different stress patterns with these sentences:

We will miss her laughter.

They must work on the project.

It is time to go home now.

Where do you want to eat dinner?

Intonation refers to the change in pitch levels you apply when speaking. In addition to just the words that you use, intonation adds additional meaning to your message. You modify your intonation depending on the type of information you are providing. When you ask a question, for example, your voice often rises at the end of the sentence. Conversely, when you are making an emphatic remark or want to sound authoritative, you usually drop your pitch. When a speaker is relaying general information, pitch tends to stay about the same at the end of a sentence, but it may rise when a word in the sentence is emphasized. These variations in intonation patterns give listeners cues that can add to what you say to them. They can understand what you are saying in part by listening to how you sound when you're talking. Here are some examples of how you change or modify your pitch level for different types of meaning:

Pitch Level	Purpose	Effect
Stays the same	Making statements	Neutral and straightforward
Rises	Asking a question	Doubt or uncertainty
Lowers	Giving a directive	Assured and definitive

Intonation Exercise

Read the words below and give each word three different meanings by changing the intonation of your voice.

Statements	Questions	Directives
→	↗	↘
go	go	go
here	here	here
now	now	now
wait	wait	wait
look	look	look
no	no	no
one	one	one
you	you	you
today	today	today
yes	yes	yes

Using Stress and Intonation Together

Stress and intonation work together to help clarify and reinforce what you say. Try the following exercise, noting how you stress your words and use different intonation patterns.

Stress and Intonation Exercise

Read the following sentences and pay attention to both the words that you stress and the intonation pattern that you use. Mark the stress and intonation pattern for each sentence. Underline the word or words that you want to stress and indicate with an arrow whether you want your intonation to rise, fall, or stay the same. Listen to yourself to decide if you are conveying exactly the meaning that you want to get across to your listener. Here is an example:

What *time* can we get a ride home? ↗

What time can we get a ride *home?* ↗

Now try different stress and intonation patterns with these sentences.

1. Where do you want to eat dinner?

2. We should give the tickets to them.

3. He enjoyed skating in the park.

4. Do you like this sweater on me?

5. I think that we should leave now.

6. This report is not acceptable.

7. How much longer do we have to wait?

8. That was the worst movie I have ever seen.

9. We should call them before it gets too late.

10. Wait over here until I come back.

PowerExercise

Listen to your communication tape from Chapter 2 and complete this checklist. Each time you add a new entry to the tape, use this exercise to help you evaluate your vocal qualities.

	Yes	No
Pitch		
Was my pitch too high?	☐	☐
Was my pitch too low?	☐	☐
Was my voice a monotone?	☐	☐
Resonance		
Was my voice too nasal?	☐	☐
Was my voice too denasal?	☐	☐
Did my voice sound muffled?	☐	☐
Volume		
Did I speak too loudly?	☐	☐
Did I speak too softly?	☐	☐
Did my voice fade in and out?	☐	☐
Rate		
Did I speak too fast?	☐	☐
Did I speak too slowly?	☐	☐
Was my rate choppy and uneven?	☐	☐

Stress and Intonation

Did I use the wrong stress in words?	☐	☐
Was my voice lifeless and dull?	☐	☐
Did I sound like I am always asking questions?	☐	☐

If you answered "yes" to any of these questions, you may want to work on improving those qualities. Concentrate on what you think could be improved, and review the exercises in this chapter to keep you on track.

PowerSpeech: Improving Your Articulation

Articulation refers to the way you enunciate individual speech sounds. These sounds are combined and strung together to create words that give meaning to your communication. Using correct articulation lets your listener know that what you are saying is important. You convey this by taking care to be clear and deliberate in your speech. When you mumble, your listener may get the impression that what you are saying is not important, or that you are unsure of yourself. Making yourself clearly

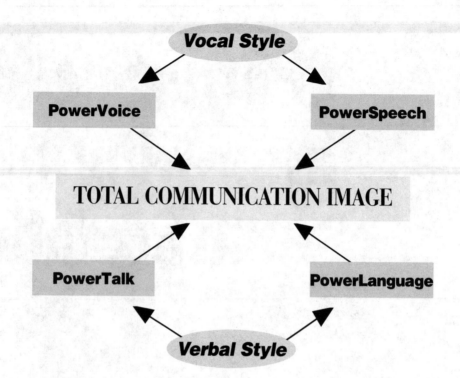

understood is essential to ensuring that you get the right message across to your listener. Improving articulation will allow you to gain credibility and avoid being misunderstood.

PowerPlan

To improve your articulation skills, you should use:

1. Crisp consonants.

2. Rounded vowels.

3. Error-free speech.

4. Correct pronunciation.

5. Modified dialects and accents.

PowerTip #1: Crisp Consonants

When you speak, you first take a breath and then talk on the air that you exhale. Consonants are formed by shaping this airstream as it is expelled from your mouth. It is the consonants in your speech that give meaning to what you are saying. When you want to be distinct and accurate, you accentuate how you make your consonant sounds. Using crisp consonants allows you to express yourself clearly so that others can easily understand what you are saying to them. Consonants are described in two different ways: *where* they are produced and *how* they are produced. The following illustration shows where the consonants fall according to these two categories.

Where Sounds Are Made	How Sounds Are Made				
	Stops		Friction		Resonating
	Unvoiced	Voiced	Unvoiced	Voiced	Voiced
Lips are together	p	b			w m
Upper teeth on lower lip			f	v	
Tongue is between teeth			th	<u>th</u>	
Tongue touches or is near gum ridge	t	d	s	z	n
Tongue touches or is near hard or soft palate	k	g	sh ch h	j	ng r y

Where Consonants Are Made

Consonants are produced by using different structures in your mouth called articulators. These include your lips, teeth, tongue, gum ridge, hard and soft palates, and jaw. You move these different articulators to various positions when you produce consonant sounds. Clear and distinct speech results from being deliberate and precise in these movements. Poor speech results from being lazy and not moving the articulators enough. Watch yourself in the mirror when you talk and make sure that you move your articulators. Ask yourself:

- Do I move my tongue?

- Do I move my lips?

- Do I move my jaw?

- Do I open my mouth when I speak?

How Consonants Are Made

You use your articulators in different ways in order to produce different kinds of sounds. With consonants, the airstream is expelled from the mouth and shaped to create the various consonant sounds. You can change or modify this airstream to create different types of sounds in three basic ways:

Stopping. The air in the mouth can be stopped or cut off from escaping. Put your hand in front of your mouth while you blow a steady stream of air without making any speech sound. You can feel your breath as it comes out of your mouth. Now, try this. Hold your hand in front of your mouth as you say the sounds *p, b, t, d, k,* and *g.* You should feel a small puff of air and then no more air coming out of your mouth. When consonants are *stopped,* the airstream is interrupted from a continuous air flow. The air escapes from the mouth in short distinctive bursts.

Friction. With friction, the air in the mouth comes out in a steady stream but is constricted or narrowed as it escapes. Again, put your hand in front of your mouth as you blow out a complete breath of air. You should feel a fair amount of air when you blow on your hand. Now, put your hand in front of your mouth as you say the sounds *f, v, th, s, z, sh, ch, j,* and *h*. You should still feel air coming out of your mouth with these sounds, but the amount of air should be much less than what you felt when you merely blew on your hand. Consonants made with *friction* allow air to be steadily released from your mouth in smaller amounts than just blowing with an open mouth.

Resonating. Consonants made via resonating are produced by air being vibrated in the spaces of the mouth, throat, and nasal cavities. By moving your articulators to different positions, you can change the size and shape of these cavities, thus altering the sound that you hear. When you make different movements like rounding your lips, dropping your jaw, or changing the position of your tongue, you create different kinds of resonance. Make the consonant sounds *w, m, n, ng, l, r,* and *y,* and listen to the different resonating sounds that you produce. Be sure not to use too much nasal resonance by letting too much air go to the nasal cavity.

Consonants can also differ in the way that they are made by whether or not they involve the use of the voice. Consonants can be divided into two categories, unvoiced and voiced.

Unvoiced consonants. The vocal folds do not vibrate when unvoiced consonant sounds are produced. Put your fingers on your voice box or Adam's apple while you say the sounds *p, t, k, f, s, sh, ch, h,* and *th* (as in the word *thumb*). You should not feel any vibration or sensation in your voice box.

Voiced consonants. The vocal folds vibrate when you produce voiced consonants. Put your fingers on your throat as you say the sounds *b, d, g, w, v, z, j, m, n, l, ng, r, y, th* (as in the word *the*), and *wh* (as in the word *when*). You should feel vibrations in your throat with these sounds.

PowerTip #2: Rounded Vowels

Vowels are made by letting air come out of the mouth in an unobstructed manner. Different vowel sounds are produced by the ways in which you shape your oral cavity. All vowel sounds use the voice in their production. Put your fingers on your throat as you say the vowels *a, e, i, o, u*. You should feel the vibrations in your throat as you make these sounds. You created the vowel sounds basically by doing four things:

- Moving your tongue to different positions in your mouth

- Changing your jaw position to open your mouth a little or a lot

- Rounding or not rounding your lips

- Using your vocal folds to voice or vibrate the sound

Two Basic Errors Made When Producing Vowel Sounds

Speakers generally make two basic errors or misarticulations when producing vowel sounds: insufficient duration and substituting the wrong sound. Incorrectly articulating vowel sounds lends an odd quality to your speech and may cause people to misinterpret what you're saying (or worse, not be able to understand you at all). Since vowel sounds are what give your voice its rich, warm sound, it's important to work on producing them correctly.

69

Too short in duration. The first common mistake involves not making your vowel sounds long enough. This creates a staccato or machine gun effect that makes your voice sound choppy and detracts from its pleasantness. Others may also have difficulty understanding you because this mistake quickens the pace of your speech and you sound as though you're running all of your words together. Making the vowel sounds longer by giving them special emphasis introduces a more vibrant and resonant sound to your voice. Say this sentence the way that you normally would:

He hit the nail right on the head.

Now, read the sentence again, and draw out each vowel sound.

Heee, h**iii**t, th**eee**, n**aaaiii**l r**iii**ght **ooo**n th**eee** h**eeeaaa**d.

Try another sentence. Say it the way you normally would. Then practice saying it again by making longer, more resonant vowels.

Charlene gave the recipe to me.

As further practice, try reciting a poem with vowel sounds that are accentuated. Even a simple children's song will do:

Row, **r**ow, **r**ow, y**ou**r b**oa**t,

G**e**ntly d**ow**n th**e** str**ea**m.

M**e**rr**i**ly, m**e**rr**i**ly, m**e**rr**i**ly, m**e**rr**i**ly,

L**i**fe **i**s but **a** dr**ea**m.

Substituting an incorrect sound. The second mistake you can make with vowel sounds is to substitute an incorrect sound in a word. By substituting the incorrect sound, you can say a different word than what you mean to. There may even be times when you are misunderstood because the word you think you used actually sounds like a totally different one. More often than not, however, vowel substitution is something that people commonly do yet still make themselves understood. Paying attention to this habit will make you sound better and will certainly make you more easily understood by others.

Following are some common vowel substitutions; can you hear yourself in any of them?

Do you say:	Instead of:
inny	any
rilly	really
tom	time
potata	potato
ta	to
end	and
git	get
rang	ring
putt	put
keller	color
wuter	water
burl	boil
oat	out
goil	girl
ha	her
wursh	wash
pin	pen

Practice reading these sentences aloud. Concentrate on making each vowel sound completely without chopping off the sound too quickly. Also pay attention to using the correct vowel sound for each word.

Long vowel sounds

A   **Kay** was **a**ble to del**ay** the ride to the tr**ai**n station.

E   **We** had t**ea** with **Lee** and **Pete** in the **e**vening.

I   What a s**igh**t it is to fl**y** a k**i**te sk**y** h**igh**.

O   **Fl**o **o**pened the box of **oa**ts and put it on the st**o**ve.

U   Tw**o** people kn**ew** that y**ou** would f**oo**l the st**e**ward.

Short vowel sounds

a   **Pa**t didn't know if **J**ack was **a**ngry or s**a**d.

e   **Me**l wanted to g**e**t a p**e**n inst**ea**d of a p**e**ncil.

i   **I**t was a b**i**t late to s**i**t down for a b**i**g d**i**nner.

o   The c**oo**k and the b**u**tcher l**oo**ked at the c**oo**kb**oo**k.

u   Her br**o**ther showed **u**s how to cook **o**nions in the **o**ven.

Other vowel sounds

ah   His f**a**ther was c**a**lm when the b**o**mb **a**larm sounded.

oi   **R**oy was ann**oy**ed that his empl**oy**er missed the app**oi**ntment.

ow   **Ou**r friends had ab**ou**t an h**ou**r to drive downt**ow**n.

aw   **Au**gust is **o**ften an **aw**ful time to play b**a**ll without a str**aw** hat.

er   **He**r g**ir**lfriend wanted to c**ur**l her sist**er**'s hair with the c**ur**ling iron.

PowerTip #3: Error-Free Speech

Sometimes when you use the wrong sounds, it's just a slip of the tongue or an accident in articulation. Other times, though, errors may appear consistently in your speech. These misarticulations are habits of producing sounds, not merely occasional mistakes. While correcting speech impairments may take work with a speech-language pathologist, you can correct some basic errors or mistakes on your own. Being aware of these common problems can help to improve your speech by heightening your attention to your own articulation skills. Following are some common articulation errors and suggestions for how to correct them.

Common Error:	Substituting a *th* (as in *thin*) sound for the *s* sound
	Substituting a *th* (as in *the*) sound for the *z* sound
Example:	*thun* instead of *sun*
	th *oo* instead of *zoo*
Correction:	
For the *s* sound:	Put your front teeth together.
	Keep your tongue behind your teeth.
	Do not let the tongue touch the back of your teeth.
	Part your lips in a slight smile.
	Blow gently, letting the air come out the middle of your mouth.
For *z:*	Follow the same procedure as with *s,* except use your voice when you say the sound.

Common error:	Substituting the *w* sound for an *r* sound
Example:	*wabbit* instead of *rabbit*
Correction:	Open your mouth slightly.
	Keep your lips relaxed and straight, not rounded.
	Raise the back of your tongue up between your back molars.
	Do not raise the tip of your tongue.
	Use your voice by saying *er*.

Common error:	Substituting a *w* sound for an *l* sound
Example:	*wook* instead of *look*
Correction:	Raise the tip of your tongue so that it touches the gum ridge behind your front teeth.
	Drop your tongue down away from the gum ridge.
	Keep your lips relaxed and straight, not rounded.
	Use your voice by saying *la*.

Common error:	Substituting an *f* sound for a *th* (as in *thin*) sound
	Substituting a *d* sound instead of ***th*** (as in *that*) sound
Example:	*fumb* instead of *thumb*
	den instead of ***th****en*
Correction:	
For *th* (as in *thin*):	Put your tongue between your top and bottom front teeth so that it protrudes slightly.
	Keep your tongue relaxed and flat.
	Blow air softly so that the air is coming out of the middle of your mouth.
For ***th*** (as in *that*):	Follow the same procedures as above, except voice the sound.

Common error:	Distorting the sounds of *sh, ch,* and *j*
Example:	When distorted, these consonants will sound slurpy and slushy as though you have too much saliva in your mouth.
Correction:	
For *sh:*	Put your front teeth together.
	Keep your tongue behind your teeth.
	Round your lips slightly.

For *sh*:	Keep your tongue relaxed and flat.
	Blow gently, letting the air come out the middle of your mouth.
For *ch*:	Raise the tip of your tongue up to the gum ridge.
	Say a *t* sound, quickly followed by the *sh* sound.
	Blend the two sounds together as one quick exploding sound, as though you sneezed.
For *j*:	Follow the same procedures as with *ch*, except use your voice.

PowerTip #4: Correct Pronunciation

Using correct articulation when you speak is half the battle in making your words understood by others. You have just learned how to produce correct consonant and vowel sounds to make your articulation clear and precise. The next step is to combine these speech sounds into recognizable words that have meaning for your listener. With that in mind, the second part of making your speech intelligible involves using the correct pronunciation of words. Your listener will not understand you if you do not connect your speech sounds in what is generally accepted as a standard way of speaking. This requires you to do two things:

- Use correct enunciation of the sounds in words.

- Use correct stress for the syllables in words.

Correct Enunciation of Sounds

Enunciation errors fall into four general categories: adding sounds, omitting sounds, substituting sounds, and slurring sounds. Following are some examples of the common mistakes that speakers make. Read the lists aloud to hear if you are making the same ones, and practice using the correct enunciation.

Adding sounds that don't belong

Say	Don't say
idea	idea**r**
remnant	rem**i**nant
film	fil**u**m
across	across**t**
ring	ring**a**
judgment	judg**a**ment
didn't	did**e**nt
calm	cal**u**m
athlete	ath**a**lete
drowned	drown**d**ed

Omitting sounds that do belong

Say	Don't say
lookin**g**	lookin
li**tt**le	lil
batt**er**y	battry

pounds	pound
five dollars	fi dollar
twenty	twenny
library	libary
center	cenner
probably	probly
because	cuz

Substituting one sound for another

Say	Don't say
sandwich	samwich
picture	pitcher
for	fer
cold	colt
them	dem
to	ta
ask	ax
soda	sota
and	ant
lettuce	ledduce

Slurring sounds or words

Say	Don't say
this year	thi shear
kind of	kinda
did you	didja
could have	coulda
should have	shoulda
would have	woulda
give me	gimme
want to	wanna
ought to	otta
that's when	swen

Correct Stress for Syllables

Sometimes the correct sounds in words may be spoken, but the stress or accent falls on the wrong syllable. You may get your basic meaning across, but you also may leave the impression that you're using words you don't know how to say correctly. This will detract from your credibility as a speaker. Take the Stress Test to see if you apply stress properly in the syllables of the words listed as examples.

Stress Test

Decide for each pair of words which option indicates the proper syllable to stress. Circle the letter that goes with that pronunciation.

1. a. PREFerable
    b. preFERable
2. a. HOSpitable
    b. hosPITable
3. a. THEater
    b. theAter
4. a. epitoME
    b. ePITome
5. a. EXtraordinary
    b. exTRAORdinary
6. a. poLICE
    b. POlice
7. a. apPLICable
    b. APplicable
8. a. comPARable
    b. COMparable
9. a. INfluence
    b. inFLUence

10.   a.   ACcept

       b.   acCEPT

Answers: 1. a

           2. a

           3. a

           4. b

           5. b

           6. a

           7. b

           8. b

           9. a

           10. b

Tips for Good Enunciation

Keeping in mind several basic strategies will help you steadily improve your enunciation:

- Move your articulators—your mouth, lips, and tongue.

- Say all the sounds in words.

- Say the endings of words.

- Say all the syllables in words.

- Stress the correct syllable in a word.

- Correct yourself whenever you misarticulate a sound or word.

- Make a list of troublesome words and practice saying them aloud.

- Mentally correct others when you hear them misarticulate sounds and words. Analyze the speech of others, but don't criticize them.

PowerTip #5: Modify Dialects and Accents

People may not be able to tell what part of the country you're from by your clothing, hairstyle, or personal belongings, but as soon as you open your mouth and speak, you might as well tell them your ZIP code. Although we might all be speaking the same language, the differences in pronunciations and use of expressions are numerous and distinctive.

Literally dozens of dialects and accents have evolved in different regions of the country, and each of these regions can be further subdivided into smaller subcategories of dialect or accent. Despite these many differences, four main classifications exist for dialects of American English:

- Eastern

- New England

- Southern

- General American

Each one of these classifications helps to identify the general geographic location of the speaker. If you asked people from various locations to say the word *you,* what you might hear is: ya'll, yous, yunz, ya, or even something as straightforward as *you.* A speaker from Maine will go to *pahk the cah.* Someone from New York will *cawl dere brudder in Lon gisland.* A southerner will write with a *pin and pincil,* while someone from Massachusetts will have *an idear* and a Texan will claim that *Ah nevah seyid thayit.*

The General American accent represents common speech patterns and pronunciations that are typically used in the Midwest. This speech has been the preferred pronunciation used for radio and television broadcasting. Whenever you hear a national broadcast you are probably listening to someone speak with a General American accent. It has been argued that General American speech and its use in broadcasting is making everyone sound alike and that the people in this country are losing their unique ways of sounding.

Each dialect or accent is simply a way of pronouncing words differently that has developed as a regional peculiarity. People who live in different regions adopt the local pronunciations because that's what they're exposed to every day. The unique pronunciation patterns sound natural to them because everyone in a specific region will tend to use the same patterns. Whenever a person visits another region, or perhaps moves there permanently, the new local speech may seem odd at first. What usually happens, though, is that the newcomer will unconsciously adopt the local pronunciation patterns and thus begin to sound just like his or her neighbors.

It is interesting to note that prejudices and attitudes can form around the way people speak. Do you think when you hear a languid drawl that the speaker is ignorant or lazy? Do you listen to the precise pronunciation native to some other region and just naturally assume that the speaker is smarter or of a higher class than you? It can be easy to assign attributes or assumptions to people's social or economic status based solely on what the listener decides about their speech. Further, your personality often can be conveyed by a particular way that you speak, and dialects and accents make up part of that style.

If dialects and accents are a result of where you live and of your individual way of presenting yourself, why should anyone consider changing them? The answer should come from some questions that you can ask yourself:

- Do you think that changing your dialect or accent is necessary for you to improve your communication image?

- Does your dialect or accent make it difficult for you to communicate to other people?

- Is your dialect or accent standing in the way of your climb up the corporate ladder because you do not sound like the other people in your organization?

If you answered "yes" to any of these questions, you may want to consider altering your dialect or accent. Eliminating your regionalisms may be too drastic, and besides, you may want to maintain some identification with your native region. This is where *modification* comes into play. By softening or adapting your speech, you can reduce the major differences in the way that you speak and still maintain some of your individuality. The goal is to make yourself better understood by a wider range of people, not to eradicate your style altogether.

How to Modify Your Dialect or Accent

You can modify your dialect or accent by repeatedly listening to other speakers and then imitating what you hear in their speech. Follow these simple steps:

1. Tape-record speakers who use the type of speech that you want to imitate. This may be an announcer or broadcaster on radio or television, or perhaps someone that you know personally.

2. Listen to this recording several times and concentrate on what you hear. Try to identify what sounds you are hearing and what pronunciations are different from yours. What vocal qualities does the speaker have that you find appealing? What do you admire most about the speaker's communication image?

3. Play the recording over as you imitate the speaker. You should mimic two things:

   • *How he or she produces the sounds.* What consonant and vowel sounds do you hear? Are they produced differently from the way that you make these sounds?

   • *How he or she produces the words.* Study how these words are produced in connected speech. Copy the speaker's style of speech by imitating his or her vocal patterns—pitch, resonance, volume, rate, intonation, and stress.

4. Make a recording of your speech using this new dialect. Listen to this tape carefully and compare how closely you can imitate your role model. Keep listening to each tape recording that you make of yourself. This will allow you to become accustomed to hearing your new style. Soon you'll feel comfortable with this new style of speaking.

PowerExercise

Improving your speech takes time and effort. Listen to yourself and identify anything that you might have to correct or improve. Making yourself understood takes clear and deliberate articulation of both consonants and vowels.

Read aloud the following lists of words and sentences. Record yourself on a tape recorder so that you can listen several times while you evaluate your speech. Be sure to make the recording in a room that is free from distractions. If you are using a separate microphone, position it several inches from your mouth to avoid any distortions in the recording. Use the Analyzing Speech Production Checklist to critique your overall speech. You should repeat this exercise periodically to monitor your progress in improving your speech.

Sounds in Words

Sound	Beginning of Words	Middle of Words	End of Words
p	pear	apple	lamp
b	bear	cabin	tub
t	time	letter	feet
d	dig	candy	mud
k	corn	monkey	make
g	gum	wagon	bug
f	face	office	leaf
v	vest	even	stove
m	money	camera	team
n	neck	banana	line
ng	—	ringing	long
th	thumb	toothbrush	teeth
th	that	brother	bathe
s	sun	poster	juice
z	zebra	puzzle	maze
sh	shell	washing	bush
ch	chip	beachball	peach
j	jump	pigeon	badge
r	rabbit	carrot	four
l	lettuce	balloon	meal
h	hand	behind	—
y	yes	onion	—
w	weed	flower	—
wh	when	anywhere	—

Sounds in Sentences

p   Peter sipped pineapple juice from his purple cup.

b   The baby used a bib to eat bananas and beets.

t   Tom put butter on his sandwich of toast, lettuce, and tomatoes.

d   Debbie brought candy and soda to the neighborhood party.

k   The kangaroo and the raccoon were walking in the park.

g   Doug began to chew his gooey gum.

f   Frank went to the doctor's office because he had a cough.

v   Victor had seven buttons on his vest.

m   Mary bought a hammer and a broom.

n   Nancy had neither a penny nor a token.

ng The king was singing for a long time.

th Thad brushed his teeth with toothpaste.

th That is his brother over there with the smooth hair.

s   Sally decided that it was safe to take the bus.

z   The zoo keeper was busy finding a cage for the bees.

sh Sheila brushed her shiny hair with a brush.

ch Charlie ate chocolate chip cookies in church.

j   George put the pigeon in the cage.

r   Randy tore his purple shirt at the party.

l   Tell me when I can blow up the little yellow balloon.

h   He was happy to hear about the trip to Ohio.

y   You can use the egg yolk in the recipe.

w   Willy went to town with his wagon.

wh They were deciding when and where to go on vacation.

Analyzing Speech Production Checklist

Use this form to analyze your speech. For each question, choose the number that most closely rates how you think you sound. Total your score to see how you rate yourself.

1=Poor   2=Fair   3=Average   4=Good   5=Excellent

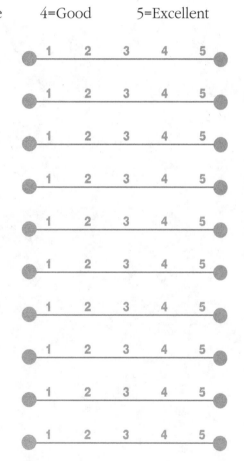

1. My articulation was clear and easy to understand.

2. I used sounds at the beginning of words.

3. I used sounds in the middle of words.

4. I used sounds at the end of words.

5. My consonants were clear and distinct.

6. My vowel sounds were rounded and resonated.

7. My speech was free of articulation errors.

8. I spoke fluidly without slurring words.

9. I spoke without stumbling or repeating.

10. My dialect or accent was easy to understand.

My Total Score: _____

41 to 50	Excellent	Keep up the good work.
31 to 40	Good	You are well on your way.
21 to 30	Fair	Study this chapter and you'll get there.
0 to 20	Need For Improvement	You came to the right place.

PowerLanguage: Improving Your Language Skills

When you communicate, the specific words that you use can either enhance or detract from your message. Sometimes just by the way you phrase a comment you can cause confusion or hurt someone's feelings. Happily you also might cause something positive to happen. PowerLanguage deals with *what* you say when you communicate, the *content* of your message.

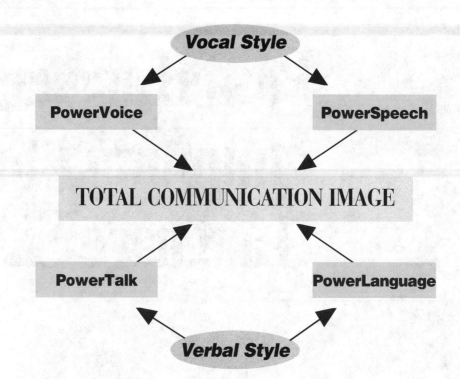

Being careful with language helps you avoid using the wrong words that can produce exactly the opposite of what you want. You can persuade people to accept your point of view merely by the language that you choose. Effective language not only makes you a better communicator; it also offers a statement about you to others. Appropriate, effective language indicates that you know how to express yourself while at the same time being sensitive to the feelings of others.

PowerPlan

To improve your language skills, you should use:

1. Positive language.

2. Easy-to-understand language.

3. Nonverbal communication.

4. Appropriate vocabulary.

5. Correct grammar.

PowerTip #1: Use Positive Language

Using positive language means verbally putting your best foot forward. You demonstrate that you know how to get your point across by selecting the right words and using those words effectively. By stating your ideas or opinions in a positive way, you can give your communication image a powerful boost. Listeners will perceive you as a person who knows what to do and how to get the job done. Positive language involves knowing which words work and which ones to avoid.

You use positive language to make good things happen, not to *react* to what happens around you. Positive language entails a combination of skills that helps you use language effectively. Descriptions of these follow.

Use Assertive Language

Assertive language demonstrates that you have respect for yourself as well as for your listener. As an assertive speaker, you avoid aggressive language that can bully or alienate people. Similarly, you also avoid passive language, which can leave your listeners thinking you're uninvolved or just don't care about the topic of conversation. Being an assertive speaker requires that you take responsibility for your feelings and opinions and express them in a direct and positive way. To be an assertive speaker, follow these simple tips:

- **Use "I" statements.** Use the pronoun *I* instead of *you*. Your purpose in your statements should be to express how you feel about something and how it affects you. This establishes ownership of what you say. Assertive speakers always express their thoughts in terms of how they view a situation. You should too.

  Example:

  Your co-worker is late *again* for your weekly staff meeting.

  Instead of:

  "*You* make me mad when you are late for our meetings."

  Try:

  "*I* am annoyed when you are late for our meetings."

- **Be specific.** Using vague statements will not get your point across. Further, you'll end up sounding like you don't have a firm grasp on the topic. Giving criticism or suggestions to others can sometimes be a sensitive issue, but as an assertive speaker you should include specific information to support your observations. Making vague remarks about someone or something does not provide the necessary detail on what improvements or changes could be made. You want to create the image that you have definite ideas and know how to express them clearly.

Example:

Your co-worker asks for your reaction to his presentation.

Instead of:

"That presentation that you made was dull."

Try:

"Your presentation could have been improved with more visuals that showed diagrams and charts to support your facts."

- **Ask for information.** You are always in a better position to make comments or responses to others if you have a complete understanding of a situation. If you are not sure of all the facts, you cannot have a clear picture of the discussion topic. Being assertive means that you should welcome the opportunity to learn new things and expand your knowledge. Assertiveness lets you be open to someone else's ideas and seek the answers that you need to improve or change. Assertive language allows you to ask for information or assistance without sounding defensive. When your listeners hear this type of language, they will be more than willing to give you advice.

Example:

Your co-worker offers a negative evaluation of your report.

Instead of:

"If you don't like my report, then you don't have to read it!"

Try:

"You said that you didn't like the report. What would you suggest that I do to make it better?"

- **Demonstrate respect.** Assertive language affords you the opportunity to ask others to listen to what you have to say. It also informs them that what they have to say bears equal importance. You should convey that you're as willing to listen as you are to talk. This exchange must occur, however, in an atmosphere where there is mutual respect and opportunity for both sides to express opinions.

Example:

Your friend interrupts when you are trying to explain what you think should be the solution to a problem.

Instead of:

"Would you shut up until I'm finished? I don't like to be interrupted."

Try:

"I'd appreciate it if you would let me finish what I have to say. Then I'd be very interested in hearing what you would suggest as a possible solution."

Make Statements, Not Apologies

If you step on someone's foot, by all means say you're sorry. Otherwise, don't make it a habit of beginning your comments with "I'm sorry, but I have a point to make." Apologizing for what you have to say creates an image either of uncertainty or of fear that your statements are not really valid. An apology should be used for what it is intended: an attempt to reconcile for some wrong doing. It should not become a standard prelude for your thoughts and opinions; you are entitled to say what those are. If you appear to doubt yourself when you talk, chances are others will too. Don't purposefully detract from what you have to say. Avoid using opening qualifiers like these:

- This may be stupid, but …

- I don't know if this will work, but …

- Maybe you already thought of this, but …

- I'm probably wrong for saying this, but …

- You may think this is crazy, but …

- I don't suppose you would want to …

Be Tactful

Just because you won't be apologizing all the time doesn't mean you can turn loose like a verbal battering ram. Sometimes communication can be hindered because the wrong word creates such a negative impression that the listener's defenses go up before the message gets through. Communication should be an *exchange,* not an assault or a wrestling match. Think about how you feel whenever you hear emotionally laden language such as the following:

- You *must* do this now.

- You *should not* do that.

- You *will not* do this.

Other words can be perceived as so judgmental in nature that they can create "hot spots" for listeners. When people hear these words, they may get so defensive they do not listen to what follows. Don't turn your listener off before you get a chance to complete your message. Be careful how you use descriptive and evaluative words like these:

dumb

lazy

stupid

fat

poor

lousy

weak

failure

awful

inferior

never

waste of time

liar

You also have your own set of verbal "soft spots" that you don't like to talk about to just anyone, topics that are so personal or controversial that they don't belong in general conversation. Always try to avoid poking into someone else's soft spots as well. If a subject is a sensitive one, or if you're not sure, leave it alone until someone else brings it up. Don't be caught with your foot in your mouth by asking one of these gems:

• So, why did you get divorced?

• How come you never had any children?

- Why were you fired from your last job?

- How much money do you make?

A word of advice: Even if someone brings up a soft spot in conversation, you may be better off just listening and not making a comment!

Ask Real Questions

You need to be sensitive in your quest for knowledge, of course, but basically your questions should be direct and to the point. Keep these simple rules in mind before you start making inquiries.

- **Ask questions for essential information.** Although this may sound pretty basic, too often people ask questions that are peripheral or unrelated to the information they actually need. Some people like to get your attention by asking a lot of questions and will fire away a mile a minute. This is usually a waste of time and can be an annoyance to the person who has to answer the bombardment, particularly if the questions are unnecessary.

- **Do not ask leading questions.** This is also known as fishing for information. If you already know the answer to a question, don't ask it just to find out if the other person knows it as well. If you want to find out what someone else thinks about a topic, just ask. Don't beat around the bush with pointless questions that make you sound like a trial attorney.

- **Do not ask loaded questions.** A loaded question makes the recipient feel as if he or she has no choice in responding without having to pay some penalty. Suppose a co-worker says, "You still don't want me to submit this report to the boss, do you?" Your choices appear rather limited. If you answer "yes," the response will likely be, "You're kidding—this report isn't good." If you answer "no," then the report will not be submitted, but is that what you really wanted to happen? Asking loaded questions presents an unfair way to manipulate someone into answering in a predetermined way. Ask your questions in a manner that allows an honest response.

Think About What Others Will Hear

Even with the best of intentions, what you say can be taken the wrong way. Sometimes what others actually hear is what you *don't* say. Be careful about how you phrase your comments so you don't create the wrong impression. From time to time, try to put yourself in the other person's shoes and think about how your comments sound.

What you say	What others may hear
Gee, you look terrific today.	You usually don't look that nice.
You're lucky you can wear clothes like that.	You look ridiculous.
You seem to be improving.	Your performance is lousy.
Are you having an off day today?	You're a real pain in the neck.
You may be more comfortable working somewhere else.	Why don't you leave me alone?

Using positive language takes practice in learning new patterns of speaking. When you hear negative statements, consider them an opportunity to break out of old habits of responding. If you're not sure what to say, write your statement down and take a look at it. Sometimes seeing your words in written form will help you eliminate certain undesirable ways of talking. With some thought, you can think of a better way to use language for positive results. To get you started, try to reword the statements provided in the Language Options exercise on the next page.

Language Options

Negative	Positive
1. You make me feel embarrassed when you talk like that to me in front of your friends.	1. _____ _____
2. This is probably a stupid idea, but could we review the project goals before the next meeting?	2. _____ _____
3. Your idea is a waste of time.	3. _____ _____
4. You don't want me to do the laundry now, do you?	4. _____ _____
5. You look like you have lost a little weight.	5. _____ _____

Add your own:

_____   _____

_____   _____

_____   _____

_____   _____

PowerTip #2: Easy-to-Understand Language

Joe: I just got a new vehicle.

Bill: Oh yeah? What kind of vehicle is it?

Joe: A car.

Bill: Is it a two-door or a four-door?

Joe: A two-door.

Bill: What color is it?

Joe: Red.

Bill: Is it a hardtop or a convertible?

Joe: A convertible.

Bill: When you said you "got" it, did you mean you bought it or leased it?

Joe: I bought it.

Bill: (Sigh) Why didn't you just say that the new car you bought is a two-door, red convertible?

All the fancy language in the world will do you no good if you can't be easily understood. Clarity in your speech means that you present enough information that your listener can understand exactly what you mean without having to root around for more details. Being as precise as possible will help you avoid misunderstandings because you make your position clear the first time around. To be easily understood, you should pay attention to your language usage so you convey the appropriate details, amount of information, organization, and structure when you speak.

Accurate Details

Good communication stems from accurate language that clarifies the message and provides all the necessary information. Things obvious to you may not be so to someone who doesn't have the full details. Tell people what you want them to know as completely as you can, using the following tips to accomplish that:

- **Be as accurate as possible.** Be precise when providing information. Everyone makes mistakes, but many can be avoided by just paying attention to details. And little details add up to big ones. Who knows, it may mean the difference between your plane ticket reading Paris, Texas or Paris, France.

- **Be specific in what you say.** If something has a name or term, use it, not "thingamajig" or "whatchamacallit." Learn the terminology associated with your job or activity. Being specific shows that you pay attention to details and are on the ball.

- **Avoid vague words.** Words that "sort of hit the mark" are of no use to you if a more explicit word exists instead. If your boss tells you that your project will be needed soon, what does that mean? Right away? Before you leave work at the end of the day? Tomorrow morning? In a few days?

Your guess is as good as anyone else's. You will probably have to ask to find out exactly when *soon* will arrive. Avoid forcing someone to ask you, "What do you mean by _____?"

Here are some examples of words that may be vague as well as how to restate the idea more specifically.

Vague Terms	More Specific Terms
frequently	daily or hourly
a substantial increase	ten percent increase
a slight charge	twenty-five dollar charge
sloppy writing	misspellings and inaccurate grammar
a few customers	four customers
a short wait	a ten-minute wait

Adequate Amount of Information

You don't need massive amounts of words to make your point. Lincoln's Gettysburg address contained only 268 words, yet the sentiment of that speech has endured well over a century. Streamlining your message makes you appear efficient. You want to give the impression that you can cut right to the heart of things, not wander around in a verbal maze.

These days people have so much on their minds that the time they have to listen may be measured in seconds, not minutes. There is so much going on that attention spans seem to last only nanoseconds. When providing information, tell as much as you need to in order to cover the topic, but don't tell every detail that you know. Excessive wordiness will have people looking at the clock as though they need to catch a bus, or worse yet, it will put them to sleep. Cut the fat and leave the meat of what you want to impart. Be brief and to the point, and your listeners will thank you.

Don't say:

At the present time it may be necessary for all of us to come to the conclusion that the project needs to be reimplemented due to the fact that it may contain inaccuracies.

Do say:

We need to redo the project now to correct any errors.

Good Organization

Have you ever been in a situation where someone tried to communicate but just jumped from point to point like a moth fluttering around a light? Frustrating, wasn't it? Organize your information and put facts in the proper order so that listeners can easily follow and understand what you are saying. Make a verbal road map so your audience doesn't get lost or confused. Before you attempt to present a number of details to someone, take a few minutes to list what you need to say. Next, check your sequence, to make sure the information flows from point A to point B and so forth. This is an especially effective strategy if you need to convey your information over the telephone. You can use index cards to help you get all the facts in the right order by following these simple steps:

1. Write a single point or fact on each index card.

2. Spread out the cards and study the information.

3. Put the cards into categories or patterns.

4. Outline the information and make additional notes.

5. Use this outline as your guide when you present your ideas.

Use Clear Structure When You Speak

Sometimes you can use the right words and have all the right information, but the phrasing you choose may obscure the point. State your information as clearly as you can. Remember, you know what you're talking about, but your listener doesn't. Don't leave someone wondering what you meant by your remarks. As a general rule, keep the message as simple and as straightforward as you can. Fancy language adds nothing if it jumbles things up. The two structures in particular that you should try to avoid:

- **Confusing syntax.** You can garble your message with syntax that is confusing or convoluted. Consider the following sentence:

  Jerry told Ron that the dentist's office called and said his X-rays showed some cavities.

  Who has the cavities—Jerry or Ron? Use plain English and simple sentence structure. Make sure you make the proper references so that people can follow what you're saying.

- **The passive voice.** The passive voice can be confusing because the verb will refer to something or someone in another part of the sentence, and sometimes this reference is not clear. Active voice is usually easier to understand because it employs action words that directly follow the person or persons doing the activity. When you speak, cast your message in the active voice.

  Passive voice:

  The study that *was conducted* by the researcher showed that people are more productive when music *is listened to* while they work.

  Active voice:

  The researcher *conducted* a study that showed listening to music while working *makes* people more productive.

PowerTip #3: Nonverbal Communication

You'd think that when it comes to communication, the words you choose comprise the most important part. That, according to researchers, is not true. At least two-thirds of what you communicate is transmitted nonverbally. Invariably what you communicate is largely a visual event. What your nonverbal signals communicate can often overwhelm the auditory message.

Purpose of Nonverbal Communication

For years, defense attorneys have recognized the importance of nonverbal communication. They advise clients on how to dress, maintain posture, and use facial expressions and gestures to convey the most advantageous message to the jury. Surely a defendant charged with a violent crime would not be wise to show up in court inappropriately dressed and then slouch in the chair looking mean. In this situation, such nonverbal behavior would not convey a message of probable innocence.

Nonverbal communication is something you do automatically whether or not you are aware of it. The key is to consciously think about what you're doing nonverbally and how you can make it work to your advantage. Though most of us are not usually aware of our nonverbal communication, you must tune into what you're saying nonverbally to give your whole message more impact. Nonverbal communication can accomplish the following:

- **Enhance the verbal message.** You give directions to someone and also point in the same direction. Your physical actions help to emphasize what you say.

- **Detract from the verbal message.** Your listeners are so busy watching all your body movements flailing around that they can't pay attention to what you are saying.

- **Conflict with the verbal message.** Sometimes you can say one thing but leak out your true feelings nonverbally. You smile when your rival gets the promotion, but your hands are clenched.

- **Regulate conversation.** Someone starts to interrupt you in conversation, so you hold up a finger and smile while continuing to talk. You let them know nonverbally that you are not finished talking.

- **Convey emotions.** Sometimes it's hard to find the right words to express how you feel, so you give a smile, a knowing look, or a shrug of the shoulders to convey what words cannot.

Types of Nonverbal Communication

There are many different kinds of nonverbal communication that you can use individually or combine to transmit meaning. A number of conduits exist to get your point across without having to rely exclusively on words. Following are some of the ways your nonverbal communication can do the talking for you.

Facial Expressions

The face is one of the most exercised parts of the body, and with good reason. Your face gets a workout whether you're talking or listening. With your face you can show a variety of emotions, ranging from happiness (smiling) to disapproval (crinkling your forehead) to fear (widening your eyes). Usually someone can tell what mood you're in just by looking at your face. Therefore, be sure that your face is saying what you want it to say.

Eye Contact

"Here's looking at you" is no joke in nonverbal communication. Eye contact signals that you are communicating directly to someone, not to the floor or another person standing ten feet away. Look at the person you're talking to, because if you don't, you may appear to be hiding something. At the other extreme, of course, don't bore holes into the person's head. Glancing away for a few seconds and then returning the gaze is a natural way to maintain contact without being overbearing. When you're talking to a group of people, establish eye contact with everyone, looking from person to person for about three to five seconds each.

Gestures

Gestures serve for more than hailing a taxi or waving good-bye. Effective gesturing helps to punctuate or accent what you say. Relaxed hand movements that complement your words are an asset to your communication. Jabbing your finger in someone's face, twisting your hair into pretzel shapes, or clenching your fists, however, will have listeners concentrating on what your hands will do next, not on what you're saying. Another nonverbal gesture to avoid is excessive nodding of your head. While nodding shows you are following the message or even agreeing with someone, too much can make you look like your head is ready to fall into your lap.

Posture

The way you position your body can send a message that you are open or closed to someone or to the topic of conversation. Traditionally, folding your arms across your chest or crossing your legs and angling your body away from someone was thought to be defensive behavior. It may be, however, that you're just comfortable that way. Body language is not an exact science where a movement or position means something absolutely. But you can use posture to appear relaxed and open to others.

Clothing

Maybe clothes don't make the person, but they sure speak volumes. Image consultants will tell you that how you dress can project a certain style or image. Individuality is fine, but watch where and how you express your personal taste in clothes. At the office, or particularly during a job interview, aim to model the company image. Your clothes will show that you can easily fit into the situation and be successful.

Time

Time is a commodity, and how you use it says something about you. Are you the type of person who always keeps others waiting? When you talk to someone, do you keep looking at your watch as though a train might be rolling through at any moment? Be sure to allow sufficient time when you communicate. If you drag things out and waste time, you will annoy others and come across as self-centered. If you don't spend enough time in conversation, you could be perceived as abrupt and rude.

Touch

In today's society, touch is a touchy subject. If you have a relationship with someone, the use of touch can convey warmth and caring. But in the workplace, touch is usually not acceptable because it can be misunderstood so easily. You're better off if you limit touching to a simple handshake. Firmly grip someone's hand and gently shake it up and down a few times. Remember, a handshake should not feel like arm wrestling, nor should it feel like a limp dish rag. Keep your grip solid, and don't forget to back up your handshake with some eye contact.

Space

People have different comfort levels when it comes to space. Generally, in the United States, a distance of eighteen inches to three feet is considered acceptable for general conversation. Of course, the better you know someone, the more comfortable you are being close to him or her. If you walked into a theater that was about a quarter filled, you probably wouldn't sit down right next to someone you didn't know. If you did, the person would probably move to another seat. Remember that personal needs for spatial territory can differ, so try not to violate another's space requirements. Different cultures have different perceptions of what is considered appropriate, so keep this in mind when communicating with a person from another country. If someone leans closely into your face, it may not be intended as either intimate or aggressive—it may just be the distance at which people communicate comfortably in his or her culture.

After thinking about these aspects of nonverbal communication give yourself a chance to observe what you've learned by completing the Nonverbal Exercise.

Nonverbal Exercises

1. The next time you talk to a friend on the telephone, watch yourself in the mirror. You may notice that you have facial habits that you never knew about. Record your observations here:

_____

_____

_____

_____

2. Watch part of a television show with the volume turned off. Try to guess what is going on and what emotions are displayed. What assumptions do you make based on the different types of nonverbal communication? Record your observations here:

_____

_____

_____

_____

_____

_____

3. Deliberately change an aspect of your nonverbal communication and observe other people's reactions. For example, dress completely differently than you normally do. Use different gestures or try using space in a creative way. Making a study of nonverbal communication will help you become more observant and to think about how you can use this form of communication in new and exciting ways. Record your observations here:

_____

_____

_____

_____

_____

_____

_____

PowerTip #4: Appropriate Vocabulary

Improving your language skills also includes improving your vocabulary. Developing your vocabulary will give your language versatility and allow you to express yourself with exactly the right words for any situation.

Use Varied Vocabulary

Emily: I *really* wanted to get that promotion because I *really* need some extra cash because I *really* have a lot of bills to pay. Besides, I *really, really* worked hard for it.

Thomas: Really?

Habitual expressions can become so ingrained that without even knowing it you can sound like you have a vocabulary of a hundred words. Vary the words and expressions you use so your listener doesn't hear the same thing over and over again. If you respond "Oh, cool" to everything someone says, you will come across as dull and unimaginative. Here's a sample of words and expressions that should be used sparingly. Remember, less is more.

Truthfully

Actually

Cool

Neat

Well

Yeah

Or something like that

Ya know what I mean

As a matter of fact

To be honest

I'll tell you what

What I mean is

Really

Limit Slang and Jargon

Too much slang in your language can create a casualness that may easily slide over into downright sloppy. You don't have to speak the king's English as though you are at an extended job interview, but too many "ya knows" or "for sures" in your speech will make you sound haphazard. Try to strike a happy balance between being relaxed and being careless.

A word about jargon: If you are with someone who "speaks the same language" as you and understands what a "graphical user interface" is, go ahead and use the specialized terminology. Under ordinary circumstances, though, don't confuse your listeners with terms or words that sound like gibberish or require a dictionary to understand.

Don't say:

I need to interface with my peer employees about the parameters of the finalized initiative.

Do say:

I need to talk with my co-workers about the limitations of the completed project.

Avoid Common Mistakes

People often substitute an incorrect word for the intended one. Take the Vocabulary Quiz to see if you're making any of these common mistakes.

Vocabulary Quiz

Choose the correct word to fill in the blank:

1. affect/effect

   The pesticide had an _____ on the bug infestation.

2. among/between

   Divide this money _____ the two of you.

3. regardless/irregardless

   He wanted to go _____ of the weather report.

4. with regards/with regard

   He wrote the letter _____ to the lawsuit.

5. farther/further

   He could throw the ball _____ than his brother.

6. kind/kinds

   We need to resolve these _____ of problems.

7. shall/will

   I _____ call you at two o'clock.

8. try to/try and

   When will they _____ fix the flat tire?

9. can/may

   _____ I go with you to the movie?

10. good/well

    He was surprised at how _____ she rode the horse.

Answers:

1. effect
2. between
3. regardless (irregardless is not a word)
4. with regard
5. farther
6. kinds
7. will
8. try to
9. may
10. well

PowerTip #5: Correct Grammar

People may overlook your bad manners, but not your bad grammar. Making grammatical errors in your speech can seriously erode your credibility. Your educational level will seem to slip a notch if you don't speak correctly. Pay attention to using correct grammar—you want your listener to be thinking about the meaning of your message, not the fact that you used the wrong verb or pronoun. Take the Grammar Quiz to determine your current skill levels.

Grammar Quiz

Decide whether these sentences are correct or incorrect.

	Correct	Incorrect
1. **Me** and **her** went to see the play last night.	☐	☐
2. **Them** two boys **is** waiting for us to arrive.	☐	☐
3. She **don't** know where she left her gloves.	☐	☐
4. **Neither** of them **is** going to the movie.	☐	☐
5. I was tired so **I** went to **lie** down.	☐	☐
6. He **done** it all by himself.	☐	☐
7. They **can hardly** wait to see their families.	☐	☐
8. Michael and Joan **was** late for class.	☐	☐
9. If **I were** you I wouldn't go alone.	☐	☐
10. **I seen** that show on television last year.	☐	☐
11. **Who** would you like to go with to the museum?	☐	☐
12. She's not as old as **I**.	☐	☐
13. He wrote **hisself** a note so that he wouldn't forget.	☐	☐
14. They gave us the **most** special present.	☐	☐

Answers:

1. Incorrect (She and I went to see the play last night.)

2. Incorrect (Those two boys are waiting for us to arrive.)

3. Incorrect (She doesn't know where she left her gloves.)

4. Correct

5. Incorrect (I was tired so I went to lay down.)

6. Incorrect (He did it all by himself.)

7. Correct

8. Incorrect (Michael and Joan were late for class)

9. Correct

10. Incorrect (I saw that show on television last year.)

11. Correct

12. Correct

13. Incorrect (He wrote himself a note so that he wouldn't forget.)

14. Incorrect (They gave us a special present.)

If you missed more than two sentences on either the vocabulary or the grammar quizzes, you may want to brush up on your language skills. Your local bookstore or library will have books that can help you do just that.

PowerExercise

Listen to your communication tape from Chapter 2 or evaluate a conversation you had recently. Use this checklist to determine how well you use language to communicate your thoughts.

	Excellent	Good	Fair
Positive Language			
Assertive language	☐	☐	☐
Statements, not apologies	☐	☐	☐
Tactful language	☐	☐	☐
Real questions	☐	☐	☐
Nonjudgmental language	☐	☐	☐
Easy-to-Understand Language			
Accurate details	☐	☐	☐
Adequate amount of information	☐	☐	☐
Good organization	☐	☐	☐
Clear structure	☐	☐	☐
Nonverbal Language			
Facial expressions	☐	☐	☐
Gestures	☐	☐	☐
Posture	☐	☐	☐

Clothing	☐	☐	☐
Time	☐	☐	☐
Space	☐	☐	☐
Touch	☐	☐	☐

Appropriate Vocabulary

Varied vocabulary	☐	☐	☐
Limited slang	☐	☐	☐
Limited jargon	☐	☐	☐
Avoiding common mistakes	☐	☐	☐

Correct Grammar

Correct use of verbs	☐	☐	☐
Correct use of pronouns	☐	☐	☐
Use of singular and plurals	☐	☐	☐

If you rated any language usage as "Fair," write it down here. Reword it to make it more effective and practice saying it aloud. The next time you make the same kind of statement, you will remember to use the new and improved version.

_____

_____

_____

_____

_____

6

PowerTalk: Improving Your Interaction Skills

In the last chapter you learned the importance of paying attention to the content of your message. PowerLanguage addressed *what* you say to others. PowerTalk now deals with another important aspect of your communication image: *how* you communicate your message. The manner in which you interact with others says a lot about your ability to communicate effectively. Your communication image is influenced by how well you actually present what you have to say.

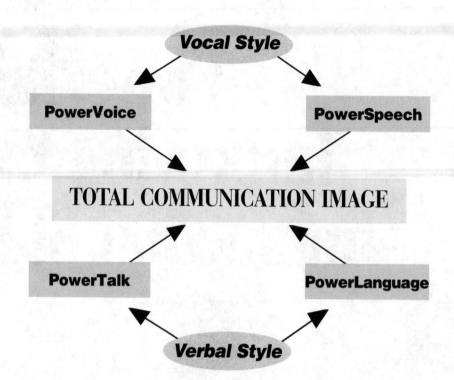

Good communication results from an even exchange between you and other people. Although you may not realize it, your lack of skills in effective talking can sometimes cause a breakdown in communication. You can't run the risk of being so caught up in what you want to say that you overlook how you say it, especially if it yields negative results. Using good PowerTalk principles can assure you that you will get your message across with a positive impact.

PowerPlan

To improve your interaction skills, you need to:

1. Change barriers into bridges.

2. Make conversation interactive.

3. Eliminate powerless talk.

4. Persuade and motivate others.

5. Meet challenging situations calmly.

PowerTip #1: Change Barriers Into Bridges

Barriers to communication are the things people do that hinder effective conversation. These barriers can create negative feelings such as hostility, anger, or resentment. Barriers drive a wedge between you and others when you create the impression that you are uncaring or uninterested in them. If you're not tuned in to your presentation style, barriers may derail your chances of sharing your ideas because your listeners may not pay attention to what you are saying.

Bridges to communication are ways that you can relate to others by making them feel special. Bridges effectively let other people know that what they have to say is important. People like to feel valued, and building bridges in conversation provides a way to do just that. The following illustrates this point:

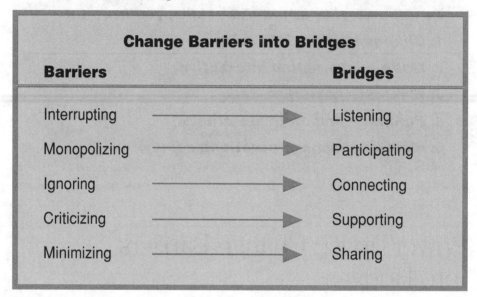

Change Barriers into Bridges

Barriers	Bridges
Interrupting	Listening
Monopolizing	Participating
Ignoring	Connecting
Criticizing	Supporting
Minimizing	Sharing

Barriers to Communication

Barriers make communication difficult and sometimes even impossible to achieve, but fortunately, with a little attention you can easily avoid them. Here are some of the most common barriers you should steer away from:

- **Interrupting others.** Interrupting gives the impression that you think your comments are more important than what others have to say. Interrupting also breaks the flow of conversation and often causes other people to forget their thoughts. It may appear that you are stealing the other people's thunder, making them feel devalued.

- **Monopolizing the conversation.** A prolonged monologue of your observations and theories will turn people off in a hurry. Avoid being a colossal bore by not falling into the "I, I, I" syndrome. Let others have their turn at talking. Most people want to share in conversation, not merely listen to a one-sided presentation.

- **Ignoring others.** People don't like to communicate in a vacuum. Avoiding eye contact or ignoring others' ideas will make them feel left out or unimportant. If people don't feel as though you accept or appreciate them, soon they will begin to avoid or ignore you in conversation.

- **Criticizing harshly.** Constructive criticism is one thing, but being judgmental or condescending in your evaluation of someone will bring conversation to a screeching halt. Sarcasm and cutting criticism will alienate others and make them defensive or even want to retaliate in an argumentative way.

- **Minimizing remarks.** Dismissive comments like "That's nothing!" or "How would you feel if you had it as bad as me?" leave others with the impression that your feelings are the only thing that matters. Telling others that their comments are insignificant or just diverting the conversation back to yourself makes you appear self-absorbed and selfish.

Bridges to Communication

Using communication bridges helps reduce the likelihood that a barrier could negatively affect the conversation. Think about these strategies for turning barriers into bridges:

- **Listening to others.** Give others a chance to talk and to finish their sentences. You will appear to be interested in them, and they in turn will feel appreciated. Let them tell you their thoughts in their own words. Don't interrupt with excessive questions or comments—that only leads to a choppy conversation.

- **Participating in the exchange.** Conversation takes team players, so be "other"-centered when you talk with people. In addition to listening, ask questions or make brief comments on what others have to say. Encourage group discussions by drawing out less talkative people and making sure they have the floor once in a while.

- **Connecting with others.** Making eye contact is a sure-fire way to show others you are listening and paying attention. But don't stop there—use any other forms of nonverbal communication you think would be appropriate (lean toward the speaker, nod your head occasionally, raise an eyebrow, etc.). Let them know that you encourage and value their statements.

- **Offering supportive remarks.** If you are asked for opinions or suggestions, do so with caution. Remember that a little criticism goes a long way, so keep your remarks short and objective. Your advice should help provide constructive feedback that will lead to improvements. Make your remarks supportive, not negative.

- **Sharing understanding.** Let others know that their feelings matter to you by showing empathy. Let them talk; then reflect back to them how you perceive their feelings. This will show that you are trying to understand what they are talking about and will help clarify your understanding of what they are saying.

Turn Your Own Barriers Into Bridges

Keep track of the barriers you may use in conversation with others. Try to examine what goes wrong in the conversations you have and why these problems occur. Think about the reactions you receive as a result of these barriers; then try to identify what you could do differently so that these misunderstandings do not continue to happen. You will notice that people will be more positive to you if you use bridges, because they will perceive you as a better communicator. This will make your conversations more successful as well as satisfying for you and others.

PowerTip #2: Make Conversation Interactive

Communication is a two-way proposition, and you have half the responsibility for making it happen. Good conversation takes time and thought, but when done right it's well worth the effort. If you invest a little energy in planning the backbone of a conversation so that it can flow smoothly, you will sound like a veteran conversationalist.

One way to improve your conversation skills is to *anticipate* what you might say in conversation. Take some time to think about what works and doesn't work for you. Reflect on some possible trouble spots. You may avoid problems later in actual conversation. This practice will help you be more spontaneous when you talk to people because you'll have already considered what you should or should not say.

A strategy that helps you achieve successful conversation is to use preplanned comments or *lines*. These lines allow you to make statements that you know will be appropriate. You thus will avoid not being able to think of anything to say. With this strategy you can pay more attention to the finer points of the conversation because you'll have built a solid foundation.

There are three basic types of lines you can use toward this end: start-up, continuation, and exit. When you plan ahead for these lines, you'll be able to guide conversation so it develops a natural rhythm.

Start-Up Lines

Conversation needs a good beginning, something to draw people in that interests them. Don't turn off conversation before it begins by using worn-out lines like "Have you read any good books lately?" Such an unimaginative approach dooms a conversation before it gets off the ground. It also immediately puts the responsibility of the conversation on the other person. Instead, invite others to talk with you by using an interesting start-up line and showing that you want to share in the conversation, not just listen. Ignite conversation with an interesting remark that motivates others to want to talk with you. An effective overture in conversation will leave others wanting more. Following are some tips for providing good beginnings:

- **Start the ball rolling yourself.** Take the initiative and check out the communication climate. It's up to you to determine if others are in a conversational mood. Use a start-up line to test someone's inclination to talk to you. Observe how he or she reacts both verbally and nonverbally. It should be obvious rather quickly if someone is not interested in conversation. On the other hand, others may not know how to approach you and will be grateful that you got things started. Begin conversation with a comment or observation of your own that will help others open up and be responsive.

  Example: Tell the person about a book you are reading and why you find it of interest or why you like that particular author. Then ask about his or her favorite authors or books.

- **Ask open-ended questions.** Ask questions that require a constructed response, not ones that can be answered simply with a "yes" or "no." Show that you are committed to the conversation. A thoughtful comment or well-constructed question lets listeners know of your interest in pursuing a conversation with them. You create the impression that you want to have an exchange of ideas and are not just making idle talk.

Example: Ask questions about what people consider the most important aspect of their jobs or what special training they need to do it.

- **Show sensitivity to others.** The fastest way to kill off conversation prematurely is to make a comment that others will find offensive. It's hard to know how strangers think about certain topics (which is why you're starting a conversation with them in the first place). Give your conversation a fighting chance by staying with topics in the early stages that are more conservative than controversial. Later you can lead the conversation to more personal topics if you get the impression that it's okay to move to that level.

Example: Ask whether the person has had any experience working with children, not whether he or she has any children.

Continuation Lines

Once the conversational ball is rolling, don't sit back and expect it to roll on without you. Stay focused on your part in keeping the conversation flowing. Let others know you're paying attention to what they're saying and you're committed to the conversation. Continuation lines let your listeners know you are in there with them and don't expect them to bear the burden of the whole conversation. Here are some continuation strategies:

- **Build the conversation.** Once the initial topic of conversation has been established, build on the discussion by asking more detailed questions. This provides an opportunity to go deeper into a topic, layer by layer. Good conversation is built on trust. Let your listener know he or she can trust you to stay with the topic and explore it step by step. You will destroy this trust if you change the topic abruptly or make a listener feel that your interest is only superficial. Jumping from topic to topic leads to confusion, and others may question why you are bothering to talk to them at all.

Example: Ask a question related to one of your listener's earlier comments: "You said that you used a spinnaker sail on your racing boat. What other kinds of sails are there and when do you use them?"

- **Keep the conversation fresh.** Although it's not a good idea to change topics too often, you also shouldn't beat a topic into the ground. Once you sense there's not a lot more to say about a certain subject, guide the conversation to a new area. A dramatic change may not be in order—you might simply shift the focus to a related area of the same topic to give the discussion a new perspective. Changing or refocusing the topic also allows you to include other people who have not said much up to that point. When you start to repeat yourself in conversation, that's usually a good sign it's time for a change.

Example: Ask, "You were describing a software package that you used to do the report. What other programs do you use?"

- **Show that you're listening.** Continuation lines prove to your listeners that you are actually paying attention to what they're saying. They will feel confident that you are listening to them and not just planning what you're going to say next. You can demonstrate this by paraphrasing or summarizing what you hear. In your own words, restate what others say to you. This lets them know that you're following the topic of conversation and understand what they're adding to it. Your comments should help provide options for new topics as well.

Example: Ask, "You identified three different ways of motivating employees on your team: flex-time, overtime pay, and a dress-down day. Which strategy has been the most effective for you and why do you think this way works the best?"

Exit Lines

Even the best conversations must eventually come to an end. Surprisingly, some people who are good at carrying on a conversation lack the skill to bring it gracefully to a close. Trying to end conversations with these people may resemble groping your way out of a verbal maze. As interesting and fun as they may be, they still may leave you wishing someone would rescue you from the conversation. If you know someone like this, or if this describes you, read on. Effective exit lines will let you gently wrap up a conversation in a way that makes everyone glad it took place.

- **Be sensitive to time limits.** Often you need an exit line because you're out of time and have to move on to other things. Conversations that run over a time limit will not end in a satisfactory way. If you are nearing the point where you have to leave, begin by wrapping up whatever you have to say. Also, don't ask questions that will require a long response. Be sensitive to others' time needs and observe their nonverbal communication as well. If they start looking at the time or fidgeting around, you may be seeing signs of their readiness to move on themselves. Using time wisely shows that you are considerate of others and respect their time constraints.

Example: Ask, "I know we're looking for solutions and our time is growing short. What do you think is the most important solution for us to consider?"

- **Recognize the end point.** When you have exhausted all facets of your conversation, it's time to bring it to an end. You may have either run out of topics to explore or conveyed all the information you needed to express about a specific topic. Sometimes, though, you realize that a conversation needs to end because you do not have all the information you need to continue. Perhaps you must find out more details or consult with someone else before you can answer questions. For whatever reason, it's important to recognize the appropriate time to end the conversation.

Example: Say, "You have given me a lot of information to think about and I appreciate your input. I have enjoyed talking with you and hope we have the opportunity to talk again soon."

- **Terminate unsuccessful conversation.** There are times when things just don't work out in conversation. Tempers can flare or the discussion takes a wrong turn into areas that cause participants to feel uncomfortable. If a conversation starts to become heated or threatens to tread on controversial ground, a graceful exit can help you avoid an unnecessary argument. Having exit lines to help you in such situations will allow you to terminate a conversation that's not benefiting either side. Be ready to close the discourse with a remark that will let your listeners know you're not going to remain in the conversation, but also that you don't want things to end on a bad note. Perhaps you should part company, but you should also leave a good impression behind.

Example: Say, "We don't seem to be able to resolve this issue right now. Let me check with Jack to get some more information and I will get back to you later this afternoon. When would be a good time to contact you?"

Complete the Using Lines in Conversation exercise to practice these techniques so that you will feel comfortable using them in conversation.

Using Lines in Conversation

Imagine a conversation that you would like to have with someone. Write examples of the three types of lines you could use in this situation.

Start-up lines:

_____

_____

_____

_____

Continuation lines:

_____

_____

_____

_____

Exit lines:

_____

_____

_____

_____

PowerTip #3: Eliminate Powerless Talk

Motorist: "Excuse me, could you tell me how to get to the interstate?"

Pedestrian: "Well, actually, um, first you, um, go down this ah street, like three blocks. And then, um, you turn left, what I mean is you kinda turn left, and then like go two, um, more blocks and, um, like you should be there, you know what I mean?"

Motorist: (Pause) "Could you repeat that, please?"

Clutter Speech

People who are good communicators say what they have to say in a straightforward manner. They waste no time adding a lot of words that do little more than clutter up their message. When you speak, it's normal to pause occasionally while you collect your thoughts and perhaps mutter an "um" or "er." This merely lets your listener know that you're still talking. These interjections are an attempt to hold the listener's attention while you search for a word or idea so you can finish what you're saying.

Clutter speech, on the other hand, is what's added to the message that does not belong there. It is speech that adds no meaning or information, but detracts from your message and interferes with your ability to communicate effectively. Speaking this way makes you sound tentative. Your listener gets the impression that you are not sure of yourself.

Clutter speech comes in several forms: sounds you make and words or even phrases that you tend to overuse. Whatever the type of clutter, it gives the listener more to deal with than necessary and tends to garble up what he or she hears. Following are some frequently used clutter sounds and words. Do they sound *very* familiar to you?

Clutter Sounds

ah

en

er

mm

um

huh

Clutter Words and Phrases

and

kind of

like

okay

so

sort of

yeah

you know

and then

it's like

I mean

or something

then he goes

or something like that

ya know what I mean

to be honest

I'll tell ya what

what I mean is

as a matter of fact

you know what I'm saying

Eliminate Clutter Speech

Sometimes you can use clutter speech and not even be aware of what you're doing. It may be necessary to tape yourself to listen to how you really sound as opposed to how you think you sound. Use your communication tape to help you analyze whether or not you use or abuse clutter speech.

Though using clutter speech can become an ingrained habit, habits can be broken. If you can't eliminate clutter speech altogether, try to cut down on these detractors so you can be more clearly understood. Eliminating clutter speech also will make you feel and sound more authoritative, and soon you will be. Try the Uncluttering Your Speech exercise to help reduce or eliminate this speech habit.

Uncluttering Your Speech

1. No Time for Clutter

   Use a stopwatch or the second hand on a clock to time yourself as you talk on any subject. Stop as soon as you use a clutter sound or word and note how much time has elapsed. You can talk about anything, from how to wash the car to what you ate for dinner last night, just as long as you don't use clutter speech. How long can you go without stopping? Fifteen seconds? Two minutes? Each time you practice this exercise, try to go for a longer period of time.

2. Write/Rewrite

   Take a sentence from your communication tape or from something that you remember saying recently where you used clutter speech. Write the sentence down exactly as you said it and read it aloud. Then cross out the clutter speech and rewrite the sentence. Practice saying this new sentence aloud. The new clutter-free speech will begin to sound natural and become a comfortable way of speaking.

   I ~~um~~ was ~~like~~ going to ~~er~~ call you ~~ah~~ last night but ~~um~~ it was too late ~~you know~~.

   I was going to call you last night but it was too late.

   Write: _____

   _____

   _____

   Rewrite: _____

   _____

Write: _____
              _____
              _____

Rewrite: _____
              _____
              _____

Write: _____
              _____
              _____

Rewrite: _____
              _____
              _____

Write: _____
              _____
              _____

Rewrite: _____
              _____
              _____

PowerTip #4: Use Motivation and Persuasion

Talking to other people is one thing, but getting them to *listen* to you is another. Getting them to *agree* with you presents the ultimate challenge. Communication is successful when an exchange occurs that benefits both sides. You can talk until you run out of air, but that will do you no good if your words fall on deaf ears. Motivation and persuasion are two strategies you can use to connect with your listener.

Motivation involves developing the desire or need to do something. Here your message will get across better if your listener *wants* to listen to you. People will become motivated to listen to you when you provide the information they need or want.

Persuasion is more than getting others to agree with you. It entails getting others to *want* to do what you suggest. Persuasion works for you when your ideas are the ones other people choose to adopt. When you persuade people, you cause something to happen.

How to Motivate and Persuade

Motivation gets people to *listen;* persuasion gets people to *act*. Here's a sequence of steps to help you motivate and persuade others:

1. Find out what people need and want.

2. Explain your ideas as completely as possible.

3. Tell them how your ideas will benefit them.

4. Ask them questions to get their input.

5. Give a rationale for choosing your suggestions.

6. Work together to reach a consensus.

For example, your boss announces to your department that he doesn't like the system currently used to evaluate employees. He has asked for input and suggestions on how to change to a better process. Using the six steps, you would:

1. **Find out what's needed and wanted.** Investigate what works and doesn't work with the present system of evaluation. Ask questions to pinpoint what kinds of procedures or activities have not been successful in the past and what would be most desirable to use for the future.

2. **Explain your ideas as completely as possible.** Providing a thorough summary of information will make people open to your suggestions. Explain what new evaluation procedures could be implemented to more accurately assess employee performance. A detailed explanation of your ideas will make your plan sound well thought out.

3. **Tell how your ideas will benefit the group.** Explain your plan in terms of what others will get out of it. People are always more open to ideas if they can see what's in it for them. What will this new evaluation procedure offer them? How will they benefit from what you propose?

4. **Ask questions to get others' input.** Ask others for feedback on your ideas and suggestions for improvement. Invite them to critique what you're proposing for the new evaluation plan. This will make them feel involved with what you are suggesting. Also, people tend to be less likely to dismiss or criticize something if they have to give a reason or justification for their ideas.

5. **Give a rationale for choosing your suggestions.** Obviously you should be prepared for any objections or criticisms of your plan. Be prepared to explain your evaluation plan, what it will involve, and how you will manage any complications that may arise. If you have done your homework, you should be able to explain why your plan is better than an alternative one. Just be sure to do this in a tactful manner so you don't alienate anyone.

6. **Work together to reach a consensus.** Present yourself as a team player and work with people to come to a consensus. Demonstrate that you are open to integrating a valuable suggestion into your proposed evaluation plan. Also create the impression that you are willing to give credit where credit is due. By allowing others to participate in your initiatives, you will gain their trust and respect. This approach is a powerful method for achieving your goals and bringing people to your point of view.

Use this six-step process to identify what you would do to persuade others to agree with your proposed ideas. You might find it helpful to write down your answers to each of these steps ahead of time so you can be prepared to meet this challenge. This will help you thoroughly think through a problem and identify the best solutions. If you do this, you'll be able to present your ideas to others and feel confident that you will persuade them. When you use this systematic approach, others will be motivated to accept your ideas and receptive to your point of view.

PowerTip #5: Meet Challenging Situations Calmly

You probably have experienced a situation like this: You are having a great day, when without warning your boss tells you that you have to make a presentation at the next regional meeting. Or, perhaps, the phone rings and someone asks you to speak at a charity fund-raiser. While your mouth is saying, "Yes, I'd be happy to make a speech," your brain is screaming, "Oh, no, anything but that!" You automatically conjure up memories of sweaty palms, a racing heartbeat, and butterflies in your stomach that felt like dive bombers.

Surveys conducted on what people fear most usually find speaking in front of groups as the most dreaded item on the list. What causes us to be so afraid of speaking in a group situation? Why do we experience greater anxiety over this than we do over the prospect of dying, disease, or personal injury? Perhaps the answer lies in the fact that fear of formal speaking represents a fear of failure and rejection. Everyone wants and needs to be accepted. Somehow, seeing yourself as failing to speak well in front of others may make you feel rejected.

How do you rate your own fear of speaking in front of large groups of people?

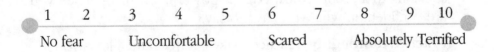

1	2	3	4	5	6	7	8	9	10
No fear		Uncomfortable			Scared		Absolutely Terrified		

Despite how much you may fear speaking in front of others, your success in whatever you do may depend on doing just that. Part of your job may require that you speak in front of groups to share information or to draw people to your point of view. Public speaking is usually defined in terms of speaking to large groups of people, but you may be as anxious speaking in front of three or four people, particularly if they have the authority to make a final decision on what you are proposing. Formal presentations, whether before large or small groups, can be accomplished successfully by remembering two things:

- **Your attitude is what is most important.** A positive mental attitude is contagious. Let your audience know that you are happy to have the opportunity to talk to them. They will pick up on your enthusiasm and be happy to listen to you.

- **Formal presentation is still communication.** You have something to say and should communicate that message to others. You are not orating to them as a performance—you are trying to get vital, interesting ideas across.

Tips for Managing Fear of Presenting to a Group

Fear of presenting to groups can be reduced by taking time to do some simple planning. Use the following tips to get yourself ready for this challenge.

Before your presentation:

- **Prepare yourself.** The more you know your subject matter and the more you are organized, the more comfortable you will feel speaking to a group. Knowledge is power, particularly when you are confident in what you have to say.

- **Practice thoroughly.** Practice makes perfect and allows you to become fluid and natural in your delivery. Tape yourself and listen to how you sound. If possible, ask someone else to give you feedback on how you come across.

- **Develop visuals.** Visuals such as transparencies, slides, charts, or even handouts can enhance your speech by providing supplemental material and information. They also may help to make you feel more relaxed by giving your audience something to look at besides you.

- **Use memory aids.** Write key words, phrases, or main points that you want to make on an index card and use it as a memory aid. That way, if you lose your train of thought you can quickly refer to your notes and stay on track.

- **Keep yourself in good shape.** The better you feel physically, the better prepared you will be to handle the stress that can accompany your speech. Being rested and feeling well helps you to think and act more clearly and confidently.

- **Visualize your success.** Run through your speech in your mind and see your success. Remember, no one is perfect, but you can still project a confident image when you give your speech.

During your presentation:

- **Challenge the fear.** Avoiding a fearful situation will not make it go away—it will control you instead. See this as an opportunity to face the fear and make it less threatening. The more you speak in public, the more accustomed you will be to the situation. Use this as a chance to grow and mature as a communicator.

- **Roll with the fear.** If you feel fear when you're speaking, let it wash over you like a big wave. Don't tense up and fight back as though you could stop it. Instead, imagine feeling the fear in your body and then letting it drain out of your arms and legs. Fear won't collect in you—it will pass through you.

- **Breath control.** People tend to speak faster when they get nervous. Steady, deep breathing will help you relax by slowing down your rate of speech. As a result, you will appear calm and collected, and you will be able to project your voice better so that everyone will be able to hear you.

- **Connect with the audience.** Communicate with your audience—don't just talk at them. Make eye contact with as many people as you can so that they think you are talking directly to them. These men and women are not the enemy; they are your partners in a conversation. (Don't forget to make eye contact with the people sitting towards the back of the room too.)

- **Inject humor.** Use a funny quote, a poem, a cartoon, or a joke to add some humor to your speech if you think it would be appropriate. Hearing people laugh with you can do wonders to make you feel less tense. Also remember to smile; others will smile back at you.

- **Project energy.** By projecting energy in your speech, you will appear more dynamic and confident than if you stand ramrod straight, clutching the podium. Moving around and using gestures not only makes you more interesting to look at, it also helps you release pent-up energy that may be making you nervous.

After reflecting on the above points, complete the No Fear Exercise to personalize what you've learned.

No Fear Exercise

List things that you can try to make yourself feel less nervous. Be creative and imagine what you could do to present yourself well to a group of three or three hundred.

_____

_____

_____

_____

_____

_____

_____

_____

_____

_____

_____

PowerExercise

Evaluate a conversation that you have had recently and think about how you have used the PowerTalk principles. This may be a recorded conversation from your communication tape or one that you replay from memory. Think about these different skill areas and analyze yourself as you really are. Then imagine how you could change or improve.

I was able to . . .	Always	Usually	Never
1. Use bridges for communication.	☐	☐	☐
2. Avoid barriers of communication.	☐	☐	☐
3. Use start-up lines.	☐	☐	☐
4. Use continuation lines.	☐	☐	☐
5. Use exit lines.	☐	☐	☐
6. Avoid clutter sounds.	☐	☐	☐
7. Avoid clutter words.	☐	☐	☐
8. Avoid clutter phrases.	☐	☐	☐
9. Motivate others to listen.	☐	☐	☐
10. Persuade others.	☐	☐	☐
11. Prepare to deal with fear.	☐	☐	☐
12. Handle fear when speaking.	☐	☐	☐

Bringing It All Together

7

Your Total Communication Image is the result of bringing all four communication components together into one powerful package. Each part of this communication model helps you to express yourself to your fullest potential. The skills you master within each of these parts contribute to the impression that you communicate effectively. When you use this comprehensive approach to communication,

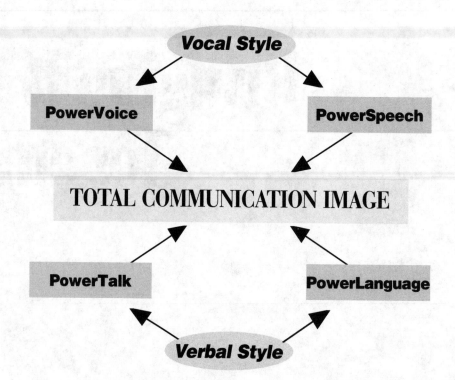

you wield a positive impact on your listeners. Your improved ability to communicate helps you become successful in whatever you attempt to accomplish.

Achieving this Total Communication Image takes dedication and focused effort, but it's well worth the work you put into it. By concentrating on integrating the requisite skills, you give your communication its strength and versatility. You become a dynamic communicator, one who can express any statement with style and ease. There is no guesswork involved in achieving this goal. By working consistently, you will gradually develop your own, unique communication image that becomes the natural way you express yourself. Your confidence in communication will grow and your positive impact on your listeners will become your trademark.

PowerPlan

To integrate all your communication skills, keep focused on your image:

1. *I*magination
2. *M*anagement
3. *A*ssessment
4. *G*oal setting
5. *E*xpectations

PowerTip #1: Imagination

Use your imagination to identify what you like about your communication, what you don't like, and what you need to change.

Listening to Yourself

Listen to yourself as you actually sound right now. Use your communication tape or pay close attention to yourself when you communicate in various activities. Identify what pleases you in your communication patterns. What vocal qualities do you use that sound most natural for you? What language practices or interaction skills are you now employing effectively? Use your present successes to build a foundation upon which to construct new skills.

Imagining Your New Image

Identify the things you are currently doing that you don't think are effective. See and hear yourself communicating well using the strategies presented in this book. Imagine what it would be like to change those things that you don't like right now. How do you think you will sound? What parts of your voice and speech will you change? Also imagine how your communication will improve when you use more powerful language and presentation techniques.

Identifying Any Obstacles

Identify any obstacles that impede improving your communication image. Is something preventing you from changing how you communicate? Are you afraid of sounding silly, or do you get something out of sounding the way you communicate now? Are you concerned that someone else will disapprove of the *new you?* Identify any problems that might diminish your chances for becoming a better communicator. Think about how you could overcome those obstacles so you can have a new communication image.

Let the Imagination Worksheet help you pull your thoughts together in this area.

Imagination Worksheet

Think about your present Total Communication Image and identify:

1. What qualities or skills you like.

2. What qualities or skills you would like to change.

3. Any obstacles that could keep you from reaching your goals.

4. What you need to do to overcome those obstacles.

	What I Like	What I Would Like to Change	Obstacles to Change	What I Need to Do
PowerVoice				
PowerSpeech				

	What I Like	What I Would Like to Change	Obstacles to Change	What I Need to Do
PowerLanguage				
PowerTalk				

PowerTip #2: Management

Learning to manage your time and resources will help you to master your skills faster and more efficiently. Use these strategies to help you organize your efforts.

Dedicating Time for Practice

Set aside time specifically to practice the exercises in this book. Change does not happen overnight or all at once—you must make a commitment to working toward improvement, step by step. Be patient and know that change will come if you are dedicated to your goals. Make a pact with yourself to set aside the time you need to improve your skills.

Sticking to a Schedule

Short, consistent practice sessions produce the best results. Practicing every day for a few minutes will yield more progress than spending an hour or two once a week. You are changing habits that you have used for years, and repetition is the key to breaking these old habits. Your schedule will keep you on track and help you avoid the temptation to skip practice sessions here and there.

Using the Checklists and Logs

The worksheets presented in this book offer you a record of what exercises you are doing and the progress you are making toward your goals. Review these notes and observations from time to time to decide where you need to go next. This documentation will also help you see what practice patterns work for you and which ones may need some fine-tuning.

The Management Worksheet provides an easy format with which to plot out your practice time.

Management Worksheet

Plan your practice sessions a week at a time. Estimate how many minutes you will work each day and on what skills. Study the overall picture of how you are spending your practice time to determine whether you need to make any changes in your schedule. Remember, it's better to practice for short periods each day than for a long session once a week.

Week of _____

	Sun	Mon	Tues	Wed	Thurs	Fri	Sat
PowerVoice							
PowerSpeech							
PowerLanguage							
PowerTalk							
Total Time							

PowerTip #3: Assessment

In order to decide where you're going, you must first determine where you are. Making these judgments helps you plan a good route to achieving your goals.

Being Objective

Don't be your worst critic—give yourself credit for having the motivation to improve your communication skills. Being unrealistically critical of both your performance and your progress will defeat you early on. Don't make sweeping judgments of all your communication skills as unsatisfactory. Focus instead on those skills that, if improved, could make your communication better. Recognize what you do well so you can build on those strengths.

Constantly Reviewing

Improvement comes in small steps, over time. By periodically rechecking your progress, you can see how your communication skills are evolving. Observing improvement will keep you from becoming discouraged. Constant review also helps you to stay focused on emerging skills so they gradually become automatic. Eventually you want to use your new communication patterns without reminding yourself of specific skills.

Tape-Recording Yourself

Use a tape recorder to listen to each new installment of your communication image. Listen critically to how you sound when you start to work on a particular skill. Carefully compare how you change with each new level that you achieve. Listening to your progress will give you a sense of achievement and keep you from sliding back into poor habits.

Use the Communication Skills Assessment sheet for your periodic "reality checks."

Communication Skills Assessment

Periodically assess your progress to identify what skills need to be developed, which ones are progressing, and which ones you've mastered. Decide for yourself how often you want to do this assessment. Doing so every month or two will allow you to see your progress. Keeping a record of how you are improving will help keep you motivated. You can also use this record as a guide for deciding what to work on next.

Assessment date _____

	Needs Improvement	Progressing	Mastered
PowerVoice:			
1. Pitch	☐	☐	☐
2. Resonance	☐	☐	☐
3. Volume	☐	☐	☐
4. Rate	☐	☐	☐
5. Inflection and stress	☐	☐	☐
PowerSpeech:			
1. Crisp consonants	☐	☐	☐
2. Rounded vowels	☐	☐	☐
3. Error-free speech	☐	☐	☐
4. Correct pronunciation	☐	☐	☐
5. Modified dialects	☐	☐	☐

	Needs Improvement	Progressing	Mastered
PowerLanguage:			
1. Positive language	☐	☐	☐
2. Easy-to-understand language	☐	☐	☐
3. Nonverbal communication	☐	☐	☐
4. Appropriate vocabulary	☐	☐	☐
5. Correct grammar	☐	☐	☐
PowerTalk:			
1. Change barriers to bridges	☐	☐	☐
2. Make conversation interactive	☐	☐	☐
3. Eliminate powerless talk	☐	☐	☐
4. Persuade and motivate others	☐	☐	☐
5. Meet challenging situations calmly	☐	☐	☐

PowerTip #4: Goal Setting

Having a plan of action will keep you focused on the right path and concentrated in your efforts. Specific goals will help you pour your attention into the particular tasks at hand.

Identifying Your Goals

As you've learned, your Total Communication Image has four main parts: PowerVoice, PowerSpeech, PowerLanguage, and PowerTalk. First decide which part or parts you would like to change—do you want to work on all four? For each part you decide to tackle, study the PowerPlan for that chapter to form an idea of what you must do to improve that aspect of your communication image.

Arranging the Steps to Reach Your Goals

For each PowerPlan there are five PowerTips to reach the goal. Decide which ones will become your work agenda. You may elect to work on all the PowerTips or perhaps choose just a few of them. Write down the steps you are going to follow to reach your goal. Arrange them in a sequence that makes sense for you.

Doing One Thing at a Time

Concentrate on changing one thing at a time. Once you have mastered a skill and feel comfortable using it in conversation, move on to the steps for a new goal. Working on one skill at a time will help to keep your attention focused on achieving the best possible results. Just remember, it is a good idea to periodically review skills that you have already mastered in order to reinforce what you have learned.

It is important to be very specific when you establish goals and the steps to achieve them. Working on the appropriate goals will give you the results that you want. The Goal-Setting Worksheet is included here with that assistance in mind.

Goal-Setting Worksheet

Choose a goal that you want to achieve for any or all of the four components of the communication model. Write down the steps you will need to take to reach this goal. When you have mastered the goal, record the date and concentrate on the next goal.

	Goal	Steps to Reach This Goal	Date Goal Mastered
PowerVoice			
PowerSpeech			

	Goal	Steps to Reach This Goal	Date Goal Mastered
PowerLanguage			
PowerTalk			

PowerTip #5: Expectations

You are working to improve yourself—so who is it you should be trying to please? Avoid getting sidetracked by other peoples' reactions and expectations.

Changing Is Gradual

The process of change doesn't happen like flicking a switch, so don't be concerned that you don't sound totally different at once. Old habits die hard, and you will have to work hard to fight them. Plateaus occur here, just as they do when you're dieting, and sometimes you'll undoubtedly feel discouraged about your progress. Don't give in to those feelings! Expect that your successes may be uneven, but as long as you continue moving in the direction of improvement, you're on the right course.

Accepting the Positive Changes

You may receive both positive and negative feedback from others as they react to the new way you sound. Remember, people become accustomed to your style of communicating, and your new image may take some time for them to accept. Allow for this adjustment and remain confident that your new communication image will lead you to success. Don't become distracted if others don't immediately support your efforts for self-improvement.

Selecting Your Listeners

Sometimes it's easier to try new skills with strangers than with people you know well. Strangers don't hold a preconceived image of you. Because they won't expect you to act or sound a particular way, they may react differently than someone who is already familiar with your communication patterns. At other times, though, it may be easier to try new things with people close to you because you feel accepted and less anxious with them than you may with new listeners. Feeling supported often gives us the courage to be adventuresome and to try new things that are challenging.

Use the Expectations Worksheet on the next page to chart the skills you're mastering and the various listeners who may be your sounding board.

Expectations Worksheet

Select what new skills you will be using for any or all of the four components of the communication model. Decide which listeners will be hearing you communicate differently, and note the positive and/or negative reactions you receive. Decide whether you want to try a new category of listeners to see what results you get from your new communication.

New Skills I Will Try   **Listeners**

PowerVoice: Family   Co-workers   Friends   Strangers

_____   ☐   ☐   ☐   ☐

_____   ☐   ☐   ☐   ☐

_____   ☐   ☐   ☐   ☐

_____   ☐   ☐   ☐   ☐

Results: _____

_____

_____

_____

_____

PowerSpeech:

	Family	Co-workers	Friends	Strangers
_____	☐	☐	☐	☐
_____	☐	☐	☐	☐
_____	☐	☐	☐	☐
_____	☐	☐	☐	☐

Results: _____

_____

_____

_____

_____

PowerLanguage:

	Family	Co-workers	Friends	Strangers
_____	☐	☐	☐	☐
_____	☐	☐	☐	☐
_____	☐	☐	☐	☐
_____	☐	☐	☐	☐

Results: _____

_____

_____

_____

_____

PowerTalk: Family   Co-workers   Friends   Strangers

_____   ☐   ☐   ☐   ☐

_____   ☐   ☐   ☐   ☐

_____   ☐   ☐   ☐   ☐

_____   ☐   ☐   ☐   ☐

Results: _____

_____

_____

_____

_____

_____

A Final Word

You have taken an important first step in a very exciting journey of self-improvement. Communication affects everything that you do, from how you deal with your personal relationships to how you handle the significant interactions that occur on the job or in your public life. Effective communication constitutes a vital part of any success you achieve. Take measures to ensure that you achieve all the success you deserve by improving your communication image.

Make self-improvement a core aspect of your lifestyle by always striving to do better. Periodically review the material that you master and add new goals to broaden the scope of what you already do well. Keep focused on continuously polishing your communication image and let it lead you into a bright future.

Bibliography & Suggested Reading

Books

Arredondo, Lani. *How to Present Like a Pro: Getting People to See Things Your Way*. New York: McGraw-Hill, 1991.

Cooper, Morton. *Change Your Voice, Change Your Life*. New York: Macmillan, 1984.

Crannell, Kenneth C. *Voice and Articulation* (2nd Edition). Belmont, CA: Wadsworth, 1991.

Elgin, Suzette H. *The Gentle Art of Verbal Self-Defense*. New York: Prentice Hall, 1980.

Fairbanks, Grant. *Voice and Articulation Drillbook*. New York: Harper & Brothers, 1940.

Foster, D. Glenn and Mary Marshall. *How Can I Get Through to You? Breakthrough Communication—Beyond Gender, Beyond Therapy, Beyond Deception*. New York: Hyperion, 1994.

Frank, Milo. *How to Get Your Point Across in 30 Seconds or Less*. New York: Pocket Books, 1986.

Glass, Lillian. *Talk to Win: Six Steps to a Successful Image*. New York: Putnam Publishing Group, 1987.

Hamlin, Sonya. *How to Talk So People Listen: The Real Key to Job Success*. New York: Harper and Row, 1988.

Hahner, Jeffrey C., Martin A. Sokoloff, and Sandra L. Salisch. *Speaking Clearly: Improving Voice and Diction* (4th Edition). New York: McGraw-Hill, 1993.

Kenley, Joan. *Voice Power*. New York: Henry Holt, 1988.

Linklater, Kristin. *Freeing the Natural Voice*. New York: Drama Book Publishers, 1976.

Linver, Sandy. *Speakeasy: How to Talk Your Way to the Top*. New York: Summit Books, 1978.

Martel, Myles. *The Persuasive Edge: The Executive's Guide to Speaking and Presenting*. New York: Ballantine Books, 1989.

Morse-Cluley, Elizabeth and Richard Read. *Power Vocabulary* (2nd Edition). New York: Prentice Hall, 1994.

Poley, Michelle F. *Mastering the Art of Communication*. Mission, KS: SkillPath Publications, 1995.

Sarnoff, Dorothy. *Speech Can Change Your Life*. New York: Dell Publishing, 1970.

Swets, Paul W. *The Art of Talking So That People Will Listen: Getting Through to Family, Friends, and Business Associates*. New York: Simon and Schuster, 1992.

Tannen, Deborah. *You Just Don't Understand: Women and Men in Conversation*. New York: Ballantine Books, 1990.

Van Fleet, James K. *Conversational Power: The Key to Success With People*. Englewood Cliffs, NJ: Prentice-Hall, 1984.

Walther, George R. *Power Talking: 50 Ways to Say What You Mean and Get What You Want*. New York: The Berkley Publishing Group, 1991.

Walton, Donald. *Are You Communicating? You Can't Manage Without It*. New York: McGraw-Hill, 1989.

Wydro, Kenneth. *Think on Your Feet: The Art of Thinking and Speaking Under Pressure*. New York: Prentice-Hall, 1988.

Audiocassettes

Cooper, Morton. *How to Improve Your Speaking Voice*. Los Angeles, CA: Morton Cooper, 1990.

Decker, Bert. *Speak to Win*. New York: Nightingale-Conant, 1985.

Available From SkillPath Publications

Self-Study Sourcebooks

Climbing the Corporate Ladder: What You Need to Know and Do to Be a Promotable Person *by Barbara Pachter and Marjorie Brody*

Coping With Supervisory Nightmares: 12 Common Nightmares of Leadership and What You Can Do About Them *by Michael and Deborah Singer Dobson*

Defeating Procrastination: 52 Fail-Safe Tips for Keeping Time on Your Side *by Marlene Caroselli, Ed.D.*

Discovering Your Purpose *by Ivy Haley*

Going for the Gold: Winning the Gold Medal for Financial Independence *by Lesley D. Bissett, CFP*

Having Something to Say When You Have to Say Something: The Art of Organizing Your Presentation *by Randy Horn*

Info-Flood: How to Swim in a Sea of Information Without Going Under *by Marlene Caroselli, Ed.D.*

The Innovative Secretary *by Marlene Caroselli, Ed.D.*

Mastering the Art of Communication: Your Keys to Developing a More Effective Personal Style *by Michelle Fairfield Poley*

Organized for Success! 95 Tips for Taking Control of Your Time, Your Space, and Your Life *by Nanci McGraw*

A Passion to Lead! How to Develop Your Natural Leadership Ability *by Michael Plumstead*

P.E.R.S.U.A.D.E.: Communication Strategies That Move People to Action *by Marlene Caroselli, Ed.D.*

Productivity Power: 250 Great Ideas for Being More Productive *by Jim Temme*

Promoting Yourself: 50 Ways to Increase Your Prestige, Power, and Paycheck *by Marlene Caroselli, Ed.D.*

Proof Positive: How to Find Errors Before They Embarrass You *by Karen L. Anderson*

Risk-Taking: 50 Ways to Turn Risks Into Rewards *by Marlene Caroselli, Ed.D and David Harris*

Stress Control: How You Can Find Relief From Life's Daily Stress *by Steve Bell*

The Technical Writer's Guide *by Robert McGraw*

Total Quality Customer Service: How to Make It Your Way of Life *by Jim Temme*

Write It Right! A Guide for Clear and Correct Writing *by Richard Andersen and Helene Hinis*

Your Total Communication Image *by Janet Signe Olson, Ph.D.*

Handbooks

The ABC's of Empowered Teams: Building Blocks for Success *by Mark Towers*

Assert Yourself! Developing Power-Packed Communication Skills to Make Your Points Clearly, Confidently, and Persuasively *by Lisa Contini*

For more information, call 1-800-873-7545.

Notes

Notes

Notes

Notes